becoming a
computer
ARTIST

author
chad m. little

Copywriting and Storyline
Gary Dulude

Design and Layout
Brian Stauffer

BECOMING A COMPUTER ARTIST

International Standard Book Number: 0-672-30397-3

Library of Congress Catalog Card Number: 93-85114

97 96 95 94   4 3 2 1

Interpretation of the printing code: the rightmost double-digit number is the year of the book's printing; the rightmost single digit, the number of the books printing. For example, a printing code of 94-1 shows that the first printing of the book occurred in 1994.

Publisher
Richard K. Swadley
Associate Publisher
Jordan Gold

Acquisitions Editor
Stacy Hiquet
Development Editor
Rosemarie Graham
Editor
Fran Hatton
Editorial Assistants
Sharon Cox
Lynette Quinn
Technical Editor
Kathy Hanley
Layout Specialist
Kim Buchheit
Cover Designer
Chad Little
Brain Stauffer
Director of Production and Manufacturing
Jeff Valler
Imprint Manager
Juli Cook
Production Analyst
Mary Beth Wakefield
Proofreading Coordinator
Joelynn Gifford
Indexing Coordinator
Johnna VanHoose
Production
Ayrika Bryant
Greg Simsic
Dennis Wesner
Indexer
Jennifer Eberhardt

A C K N O W L E D G M E N T S

To all the people that have worked so hard to create this book, thank you very much. To the many talented artists and their tireless efforts, I want to extend all my thanks for allowing me to display your artwork on these pages.

Brian Stauffer

Thank you for the many hours you spent on the design and layout of this book. Your talents are immense, almost as immense as the effort it took to produce this book. It's always a trip to work with such a visionary.

Gary Dulude

The only person with enough insight to write the story from an idea and a vision. Thank you for using your tremendous talent and abilities to bring the characters to life and put this vision into words.

Lori Simpson

Without your support over the past few years, this child would have never been born. Neither would I.

Lonnie Whittington and Jim Layne

Two partners, two friends, too much. Thank you for all the criticism, insight, and patience while waiting for this project to be completed.

Tery Spataro, Brooke Nanberg, and Kim Buchheit

Enough with the circles, Brian. Thank you for all your help in producing this monster.

Louis Katz and Kory Kredit

I hope to work with you for many years to come. Thank you for allowing me to publish your work.

Jeff Brice, Mark Jasin, and Ron Scott

Thank you for contributing your spectacular artwork — and your insights into computer art — for this book.

Computer art will never be as revered as the art created by the masters.

Anyone could create it if they had enough money for a machine like this.

Yeah, but can it do this?

Is it always going to look pixilated like that?

These young punks are going to kick my butt.

I'm not going to look.

I'm not going to listen.

But it's not going away.

The combination of technology and art is here to stay, no matter what form it evolves into. The computer is a valid artist's tool, and it will always grow — just as you will!

As you grow with the computer, you'll understand the unlimited capabilities that can expand your creativity and talents.

This publication isn't typical.

Change is an experience that none of us handles the same way. This book is the story of one person's encounter with change, after he finds a computer in an abandoned warehouse. Turning it on he unleash-

es Vincent, a computer-generated mentor who introduces him to computer art and helps him through the first tentative steps into this new medium. As the story unfolds, you will join the narrator in the art of learning — and hopefully share in his enthusiasm and excitement.

You won't become an artist.

People don't learn to be artists. They are. This book will merely show you how to use the computer hardware and

the fastest? What programs are the most cost-effective for your purposes? Knowing the evolution of computer art will help you answer these and other questions.

Don't be afraid.

Computer art isn't black magic. The computer is simply a tool — albeit a highly sophisticated one. After you've covered the basics, you'll learn how to produce computer art yourself. You'll still be using your innate talents and creativity, together with a newfound understanding for the computer's capabilities.

This is not a program-specific book.

Computer graphics programs fall into two categories, each with individ-

software to realize your creative visions. You'll see how this amazing piece of equipment — once you've mastered its power — can expand your creativity and art.

Begin at the beginning.

To truly understand the basics of creating computer art, you must follow the complete experience. Once you know where computer art came from, you'll see where it is going. Then you'll have the insight to watch the technology evolve. Whose computer will be

ual strengths and weaknesses. Most all graphics programs perform the same functions. If you need to learn about your program's specific capabilities, use the manual that came with your software. Yeah, I know; it's probably still in the shrink wrap. Even for Vincent and myself, it's usually the last resort.

You have to do it to learn it.

Pushing the button that rotates the square may be getting old, but learning by doing is the only

PREFACE

Vincent isn't through teaching, and if you're willing to learn, there will be other opportunities to explore such areas as 3-D in the future.

I can't tell you which programs to use.

Like other artist's tools, computer programs are a matter of personal choice. However, some very talented computer artists have offered their favorite tools in this book. Besides their recommendations, you should look closely at the different hardware and software products available. Do they have a broad user base? Is the company a long-term player in the market? Do the people writing the programs care about the user interface?

way to become a computer artist. Now that you know what that little button does, keep going. See what it can do in combination with your knowledge and talent.

This is just the beginning.

Vincent touches on some fairly complex subjects, such as 3-D. Remember, there are infinite facets to computer art, and this book can only present a portion of them. But

Can they help you accomplish the results you're after? Show me what it does! These criteria will determine your choices.

The proof is in the output when a talented person creates computer art. If it's there, then they've done their job. Now it's your turn.

I hope you enjoy creating computer art as much as Vincent and I.

Table
of contents

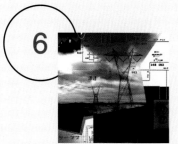
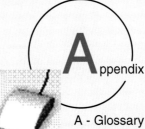

discove

compu

g

1

The old warehouse at the address the real estate agent had given me didn't look too promising at first. It bore all the tell-tale signs of neglect — peeling paint, rock-shattered windows, rotting wood in spots. Still, like the other dilapidated buildings in the neighborhood, it wasn't a lost cause. I could see its potential in the warehouses where the decay had been scrubbed away, replaced by fresh paint and new tenants.

I needed more space for my art studio, and the idea of a converted warehouse appealed to me. I liked the character of old buildings — the architectural details that chrome and glass office towers notably lack — and warehouses had the vast open spaces I wanted to create and display my work. Besides, in the world of commercial real estate, they were cheap. Relatively speaking, anyway.

My agent was late. I wandered around outside the warehouse, the artist in me considering ideas to remodel and revive it. The accountant in me was figuring the cost — who's to say artists can't have a practical side? Then I noticed the back door. It was slightly ajar, almost daring me to come inside.

Now, ordinarily, I wouldn't just venture into an old, practically abandoned building in what would be considered the wrong side of the tracks. But I didn't have all day to wait for my agent to show me around. Besides, the sun was shining, and with plenty of windows along the top of the walls — several without the added hindrance of glass — it wasn't as if the interior would be a pitch dark cauldron of evil spirits.

I pushed open the creaky back door and surveyed the cavernous interior.

Pretty much what I expected. Assorted shards of broken glass. At least a dumpster's worth of trash. Some long-abandoned empty crates. And a computer.

Wait a minute. What was a computer doing here? Surely the previous owners hadn't just left it here. At any rate, this old warehouse appeared to have been abandoned long before computers became an office staple.

Except for an unusual looking monitor, it appeared to be a run-of-the-mill, desktop computer, not too different from the one I had recently bought. It was plugged in, too.

Because my agent was now 20 minutes late, I could either leave or see if there was anything interesting on the computer. My afternoon was free, so I turned it on.

After going through the normal start-up routine, the screen went blank. Maybe the computer didn't work anymore and had simply been abandoned with the building, I thought.

As I was about to turn off the machine, though, the monitor lit up, sending a montage of color and light into the old warehouse. Then, slowly, pixels of light began to take shape. What appeared, although human in form, had a surrealistic quality about it that I couldn't quite pin down. I just stood there with my mouth agape.

"I've been waiting for somebody to let me out of that computer," the hologram before me boomed. "My name is Vincent, and I'm going to introduce you to the world of computer graphics."

I continued to stare dumbly at Vincent.

He smiled at me. "I suppose you find me a bit startling. Don't worry, I'm a harmless hologram. If you press the spacebar, we can begin the program."

Though I expected Rod Serling to tap me on the shoulder at any moment, I hit the spacebar anyway. The computer's screen flickered, then brought up a menu. One dialog box was titled *Events and Technological Advances*; a second *The People of Computer Art*; and the third *Computer Art Techniques and Theories*. With the mouse, I clicked the first box.

The menu dissolved, as did Vincent. Again, I thought the machine might have died, but a new hologram appeared. In the corner of the old warehouse, I saw an ancient computer, a huge machine that must have been one of the first ever built.

"You might be surprised to learn that graphic arts applications go back to the beginning of the computer age," Vincent said as he suddenly popped back into the image. "Some of the first computers were used to produce graphics, and many early computer scientists concentrated on graphics applications.

"This machine is the Whirlwind," he continued. "Built in 1949 at the Massachusetts Institute of Technology, it was one of the earliest mainframe computers to have a display screen like a television monitor."

3

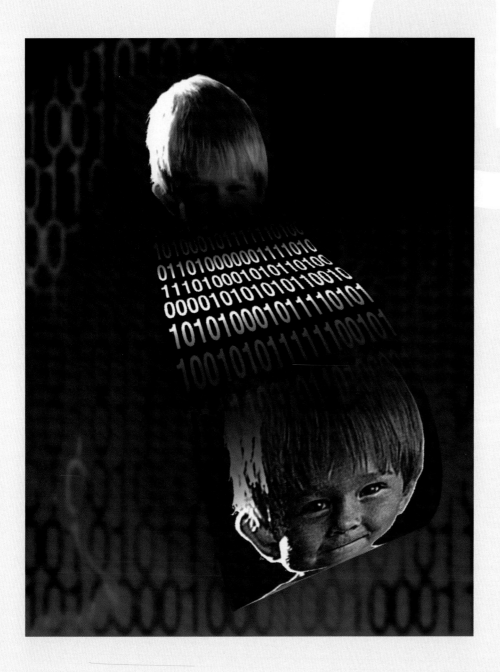

said. Then he grinned. "Yes, I can hear you, so feel free to ask questions as we go along."

Vincent then turned his attention back to the Whirlwind. "See that?" he said, pointing to a ball bouncing on the Whirlwind's screen.

"The Whirlwind and its bouncing ball showed how complex mathematical information could be displayed in a more understandable way," Vincent continued. "The Whirlwind also showed how computers could be put to practical use in a graphical format."

The hologram suddenly changed to a black and white television set, tuned to Edward R. Murrow's *See It Now*. Vincent, now seated in the easy chair in front of the TV, pointed out Murrow describing the breakthrough capabilities of the Whirlwind.

"I wonder what kind of graphics that machine could create," I muttered to myself.

Either the computer had a microphone, or Vincent had ears.

"Well, one of the first programs written for the Whirlwind created a ball bouncing up and down the screen, losing height with every bounce as though it was affected by gravity," he

The program ended with the computer playing "Jingle Bells." Even though it appeared so simple, I couldn't help being amazed how this huge collection of vacuum tubes had created a ball bouncing up and down the screen.

The television faded away, and Vincent turned his attention back to me. "I suppose you may be wondering just who I am," he said.

"Well, you have the same name as one of my favorite artists," I replied.

"Oh yes, Van Gogh," Vincent replied. "I represent the many artistic possibilities you have with the computer. Just as there are a variety of styles in traditional art, computer art varies according to the artist. As computer-generated art, I can be whatever the artist wants me to be."

"And you're going to show me some of those possibilities?" I asked.

"Of course," Vincent replied. "And you'll see the people and technologies that made them possible."

With that, the computer brought up a new hologram, this one with a man working at another huge computer. "Not long after the Whirlwind came another advance: feeding pictures into computers using a rotating drum with a photo-electric cell. You probably thought scanning was a new technique, didn't you?"

"Well, yes."

"Actually, it dates back to 1957," Vincent motioned toward the hologram, "when

"You probably thought scanning was a new technique, didn't you?"

Russell Kirsch developed the rotating drum scanning technique at the U.S. National Bureau of Standards."

"What did he scan?" I asked.

Vincent pointed to a photograph, which Kirsch picked up and placed in the drum scanner. "Kirsch's first scan was a photograph of his baby boy," Vincent said as Kirsch operated the scanner, then brought the image up on the screen. "It was the first time a computer could see the visual world as well as process it.

"Have you ever wondered how computer graphics got its name?" Vincent asked as Kirsch and his machine faded away.

Frankly, I hadn't given the matter much thought. Still, I could tell a leading question when I heard one. "How?"

The hologram that appeared behind Vincent looked like the cockpit of an airplane.

"Computer graphics applications had been around for more than a decade before they had a name," Vincent explained as he sat down in the cockpit beside another figure. "This is William Fetter, a researcher at the Boeing Company, who coined the term *computer graphics* in 1960 to describe computer-generated plotter drawings of an airplane cockpit."

"When he used the term *computer graphics*, he meant technical drawings that were produced on a plotter, like the ones used to design this cockpit," Vincent said. "It was originally an engineering term, but *computer graphics* soon became a catch-all designation, and any graphic work produced with the assistance of a computer was grouped under this confusing misnomer." He got out of the cockpit as it and Fetter disappeared.

Now, I was confused. "I thought artists created computer art," I said. "Why were engineers involved?"

"Have you ever wondered how computer graphics got its name?"

6

"Computer graphics were actually the domain of scientists and engineers for many years," Vincent said. "For them, creating graphics on a computer was a mathematical and engineering problem. Graphics were the result of the computer's number-crunching feats, such as frequency, randomness, iteration, and interpolation."

I understood frequency and randomness, though I knew of them as elements in a drawing, not in the mathematical sense. "Can you explain iteration and interpolation?" I asked.

"*Iteration* is the repetition of an operation with slight changes in each repetition," Vincent replied. "*Interpolation*, by contrast, is the transformation of one linear image into another through the calculation of a variable number of new values between two existing values."

"What?" Now I was really confused.

"Put another way, interpolation is a mathematical calculation used to create certain types of images or effects," Vincent explained. "At this point, the tools to create computer art were complex algorithms, which is why mathematicians dominated early computer graphics."

"So you couldn't just draw on the computer like you do today?" I asked.

"Actually, one man did create a way to draw interactively on the computer," Vincent replied as the computer brought up another hologram. This time, there was a man who appeared to be drawing on the screen of his computer, another big, old machine. As he moved his pen across the screen, his movements were traced by a beam of light.

"This is Ivan Sutherland and the Sketchpad," Vincent explained as we watched Sutherland draw several geometric shapes on the screen. "It was the first interactive computer graphics system, which he developed while working on his doctoral thesis at MIT in 1963."

"How did it work?" I asked.

Vincent turned to Sutherland. "Could I try that for a minute, please?" he said, pointing to the pen Sutherland had been using. Sutherland handed it to Vincent, who held it out to show me.

"This pen contains a photoelectric cell," he explained. "Any movement across the cathode ray tube was interpreted on the screen by the path of light from the pen." Vincent began drawing on the screen.

"You could draw simple geometric shapes, then rotate and relocate them," he said as he demonstrated. "Sutherland also designed the Sketchpad with enough memory to store and recall the forms."

"But Sutherland wasn't exactly an artist, was he?" I said.

"No, not in the traditional sense," Vincent replied as he handed back the pen. "You see, in order to get these early computers to do anything, you had to be an extremely experienced mathematician and programmer. Very few of them had any sort of traditional art background. And quite frankly, there weren't that many machines to go around in those days. The only people who had access to computers were the scientists and engineers at research centers and major institutions."

"So when did the art world finally start to take notice of computers?" I asked as Sutherland and his Sketchpad disappeared.

"If you have to pin a date on it, you could say it happened in 1963," Vincent replied as the computer brought up another hologram, which appeared to be an art exhibit. "That year, the

"So when did the art world finally start to take notice of computers?"

7

the artist will simply create

SIMULATED CAMERA LENS
5.13.90

F.P.O.

INSET TEAL TO WHITE GRADIENT
5.2.90

CLOSEUP ON WATER
5.17.90

F1

Proper tim

O

1/2

D

d

p

P

1/4

9

trade periodical *Computers and Automation* announced the first competition for computer graphics. The winners were to be chosen on aesthetic merit instead of design practicality."

"Two years later, computer art was exhibited to the general public in the United States and Europe for the first time," Vincent continued as three men appeared. "Three mathematicians, Frieder Nake, A. Michael Noll, and George Nees, presented the first exhibition of computer graphic art at Technische Hochscule in Stuttgart, Germany."

The scene shifted to another art exhibit. "In the United States, digital graphics were first shown at the Howard Wise Gallery in New York, gaining the attention of local art critics."

Two men appeared in the hologram, who I took to be art critics based on what Vincent had just said. They peered critically at a few of the pictures on display.

Vincent approached the two art critics. "Excuse me, gentlemen," he said. "Could you tell me what you think of these computer graphics."

The first critic looked at him with notable disdain. "These pictures," he said sourly, "not only resemble the notch patterns found on IBM cards, they have about the same amount of aesthetic appeal."

"They're cold and soulless," said the second as they walked away.

"Who were they?" I asked Vincent.

"Just a couple of art critics from *Time* magazine and the *New York Herald Tribune*." Vincent replied as if their pronouncements meant nothing.

"They certainly didn't like those early computer art samples," I observed.

"Yes, and they failed to recognize computer graphics as an art form in its very early stages," Vincent said. "Instead, they chose to criticize the tools used to create it."

"Why was that?"

"Some art critics viewed computer graphics as rigid and lacking the chaos and organic matter found in traditional art forms," Vincent explained. "That may have been true in some cases, but while computer art has evolved in the ensuing years, many of these original perceptions haven't changed.

"Didn't anybody like the exhibit?" I asked

"He did," Vincent said, pointing to a new figure that came into the hologram. "That's Stuart Preston, from the *New York Times*. Unlike some of his contemporaries, he could see the computer as a powerful creative force."

Vincent turned his attention to the *Times* critic. "Mr. Preston," he said, "do you see any future in computer art?"

Preston nodded. "When almost any kind of painting can be computer generated, from

$$E = mc^2$$

The bblank computer scren
was just like a blank canvas,
made more daunting byy its
seeminly limitless capablities.

14

then on, all will be entrusted to the *deus ex machina*."

"What do you mean by that?" Vincent asked.

"Well, freed from the tedium of techniques and the mechanics of picture making, the artist will simply create," Preston replied.

"That's an interesting theory," I said to Vincent after Preston and the exhibit were gone. "Now that I've seen some early examples of computer art, I'd like to know more about the people who created it. Can we do that?"

"Oh sure," Vincent replied. "Just press the ESC key at any time to return to the main menu. Then you can click the section devoted to computer artists. We can come back to this section where we left off."

I did as Vincent instructed, bringing up the main menu, then another menu with a series of names. I recognized "A. Michael Noll" from the 1965 computer art exhibit in Germany and clicked on his name.

The computer brought up a new hologram, this time the image of a man with two drawings.

"I assume that's A. Michael Noll," I said.

"That's right," Vincent said. "And though he was a computer scientist, he did see computer graphics as a form of art. In fact, he was one of the first to apply traditional art techniques to the computer."

"From what I've seen so far," I said, "computers generated art using math. None of the art techniques I know of are based on math, at least not the ones that I use. How could he apply traditional art techniques to the computer?"

"Well, at this point, computer graphics were still based on math," Vincent replied. "What he did, though, was apply to the computer one of the techniques art students learn, which is to create their own versions of famous artworks. You are familiar with the technique aren't you?"

"Yes," I nodded.

"If students could learn by reproducing art, Noll thought there was no reason why the computer couldn't learn the same way," Vincent explained. "And he was fairly successful in reproducing several pieces of abstract art using the computer." Vincent pointed to the prints behind Noll. "One of these," Vincent said, "was a semi-random picture remarkably similar in composition to the original 1917 Mondrian Plate 9."

After racking my brain, searching for a mental picture of the Mondrian print, I had come up dry. "Which one is the original and which is the reproduction?" I asked, cursing myself for skipping too many art history classes.

"I'm not telling," Vincent replied. "But you can help recreate an experiment Noll performed on 100 people at Bell Labs. He showed them photocopies of both the original and the computer-generated versions — just as you see here — and asked them to participate in an experiment to determine what aesthetic features are involved in abstract art.

"Noll told them to identify the computer art and the picture of their preference," Vincent continued. "Now, it's your turn. Which drawing is computer generated, the one on the left or on the right?"

"Right," I said.

"And which one do you prefer?"

"Left."

"Aha!" Vincent exclaimed in triumph. "You're just like most of Noll's subjects at Bell Labs. Only 28% correctly identified the one on the left as the computer-generated picture."

"But the one on the right is so much more orderly," I protested. "It *looks* like it was created by a machine."

"Yes, it does," Vincent admitted. "And that's why an astonishing 59% of Noll's test audience — just as you — preferred the computer's rendition of the painting to Mondrian's original. People seemed to associate the randomness of the computer-generated picture with human creativity."

"I didn't think the computer could produce randomness," I said.

"You've just hit on one of the most difficult elements of producing computer graphics," Vincent said. "Traditional art is considered organic in nature because there is an element of randomness in the image. When you're wielding a paintbrush, there's a chance that paint or watercolor or whatever is going to go off in some unknown direction. But the tools used for creating computer graphics tend to not allow for that randomness."

Now I was confused again. "If computers don't allow for randomness like, say a paintbrush, how did Noll do it?" I asked.

"Math," Vincent said. "Anything with the computer eventually boils down to math. Noll created randomness in his graphic images through algorithms, which are basically mathematical formulas for solving specific problems."

Noll turned and handed Vincent another picture. "Noll won first place in *Computer and Automation*'s 1965 art contest with this drawing. Want to guess how he produced it?"

Another leading question. "Math?"

"Bingo," Vincent said. "The mathematical formulas created the randomness."

As Noll's image faded, I began to wonder if I'd meet any computer artists with an art background in this program. "Can you show me an artist who got involved with computer graphics?" I asked.

"The computer acts as a third party because it is the tool used to produce the art."

Vincent nodded. "Although most early computer artists were scientists, engineers, or mathematicians, there were a few with a traditional art background," he said as a new hologram appeared. "Like him."

"That's Charles Csuri," Vincent continued. "Back in the sixties, he was an artist and faculty member at Ohio State University."

"How was his art different from what people like Noll produced?" I asked.

"Csuri was the first to produce computer-generated representational art in 1966," Vincent explained. "Up to this point, engineers such as Mike Noll created computer art mathematically and with programs. Csuri's compositions, however, originated as pencil drawings of representational subject matter."

"So he would actually draw something by hand first," I said.

"Exactly. Then he scanned those images, which converted them into digital information," Vincent continued. "Once the images were in the computer, he could assign coordinates to the outlines of the

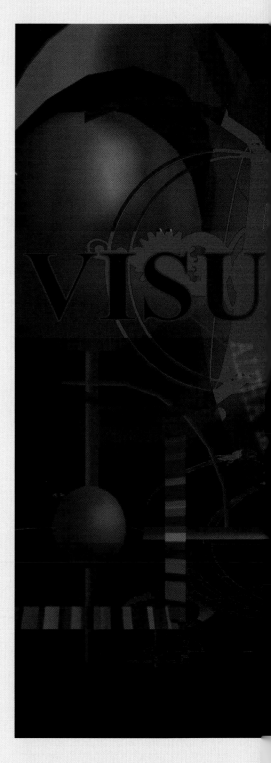

compositions and manipulate them to produce his artwork."

Vincent held out one of Csuri's compositions. I had to admit, it didn't look like some of the computer graphics I had seen earlier. "What else did he produce?" I asked.

"In addition to creating artwork on the computer, Csuri also got involved with the early stages of computer animation," Vincent replied. "In 1970, he

developed a real-time film animation program on an IBM computer." The computer appeared behind Csuri.

"IBM was so impressed with the software that they invited Csuri and his associates to New York and gave them access to equipment in IBM's main Manhattan showroom." The background in the hologram shifted again to what I presumed to be the IBM showroom. I could see people crowding around the computers as Csuri and his associates conducted demonstrations.

"For three days," Vincent continued, "Csuri and his associates manned the installation and dazzled passers-by with the powerful software."

My memories of art history class suddenly returned as I saw a familiar figure in the crowd around Csuri's computer. "Isn't that Salvador Dali?" I asked.

"So why don't vector graphics need frame buffers?" I asked.

"Yes. By this time, the computer was beginning to be seen as another tool for artists," Vincent said. "In fact, he developed this early animation software with artistic applications in mind."

Csuri and his IBM showroom exhibit faded, and the people menu screen returned. Among all the names listed on the menu, one didn't seem to be a name: EAT. "What was EAT?" I asked, curious, and now slightly hungry.

"*Experiments in Art and Technology*, or EAT, was formed in 1967 by Robert Rauschenberg and Billy Klüver at Bell Labs," Vincent explained as the computer

brought up a new hologram with two men and a bizarre-looking sculpture. "EAT was formed as more artists began to explore combinations of art and technology, like this sculpture created from radios and other examples of twentieth-century technology. As the idea of the computer as an artistic tool became more accepted, EAT attracted artists as well as scientists from such prestigious organizations as AT&T and IBM."

"So, through EAT, artists came to embrace the computer?" I asked.

"Not exactly," Vincent replied. "A lot of people, especially traditional artists, were put off by technology. Right, Bob?" Vincent turned to Rauschenberg.

"Yes," Rauschenberg nodded. "We are ashamed of technology. Some are turning their backs on it, fleeing the technological present."

As Rauschenberg, Klüver, and their bizarre sculpture disappeared, I thought about how I had resisted and put off buying a computer — and then relented only because it would help me keep better track of my bookkeeping. Like other traditional artists, I had, perhaps inadvertently, held the same prejudice against computer art.

"Would you like to know why more artists weren't involved in computer graphics?" Vincent asked.

It was as though he had read my mind. "Yes."

"She might be able to shed some light on the subject," Vincent said as the computer brought up an image of a woman and another art exhibit. "That's Jasis Reichardt, and in 1968, she shook the art world with an exhibit at the London Institute of Contemporary Art."

The combination of her name, 1968, and the London Institute sounded vaguely familiar. "Was that exhibit *Cybernetic Serendipity*?" I ventured.

"You do remember a bit of art history, don't you?" Vincent grinned at me. Her exhibit *Cybernetic Serendipity: The Computer and the Arts* confronted the art community with the radical implications of the computer. She included the computer in poetry, paintings, sculpture, robotics, choreography, music, drawing, films, and architectural renderings. All of these things, and the book that followed, demonstrated how pervasive the use of technology had become in the creative process."

"It's like Stuart Preston had said; technology can be used as a tool for the artist," I observed.

"True," Vincent said. "But at the time Reichardt exhibited *Cybernetic Serendipity*, computer graphics were still overwhelmingly produced by scientists and engineers. Most traditional artists shunned rather than embraced computer technology, afraid that computers would usurp their creativity and control. They didn't realize, as Stuart Preston from the *Times* did in 1965, that the computer is simply a tool for their creativity.

"The lack of traditional artists in computer graphics wasn't just due to their suspicions about technology," Vincent continued. "Even those artists who weren't afraid of computers had difficulties in working with them."

1

"Computers back then must not have been very user-friendly to the uninitiated," I remarked, remembering my own endless cycle of trial and error with a simple desktop machine.

"The term *user-friendly* didn't even exist in the late 1960s," Vincent said. "And even if it did, it could never have been applied to the computers of the day. Those machines still required engineering and programming expertise. The majority of artists interested in computers didn't want to be concerned with programming or creating the complex mathematical codes necessary to get what they wanted."

"It seems as though the scientists and engineers had the lock on computer graphics in the early years, and artists didn't have the technical skill," I observed. "Was there anybody who could combine the two personalities?"

Vincent looked at me thoughtfully. "As a matter of fact, there was," he said as the computer brought up a new hologram. "That's Kenneth C. Knowlton, an artist *and* a programmer. Knowlton collaborated extensively with artists Stanley Van Der Beek and Lillian Schwartz at Bell Labs in the 1960s and 1970s."

"Ken's vision for computer graphics was a combination of the best elements of programmers and artists," Vincent said. "What were those common characteristics, Ken?"

"Both groups are creative, imaginative, intelligent, energetic, industrious, competitive, and driven," Knowlton replied.

"I'll agree with Knowlton on that, but what about the differences?" I asked Vincent. "I know the stereotypes of both personalities. How can those be resolved?"

"It isn't easy," he acknowledged, "and having the computer as a third party makes it all the more difficult."

"I'm not sure what you mean," I said, puzzled.

"The computer acts as a third p. because it is the tool used to prod the art. With no programming ex tise of his own, the artist must c municate his ideas to a computer entist or programmer. The scientis programmer must then interpret artist's ideas and communicate interpretation in a form that the c puter can understand and execute

"And when you have two diffe people trying to communicate idea, something always gets lo the translation," I observed.

"Exactly. There was simply too g an opportunity for miscommur tion in the process to expect the result to match the artist's orig vision," Vincent said.

"If this was the problem, when an artist not need a programme

"We can do that," Vincent replied. "Hit the ESC key, go back to the main menu, and we'll pick up the Events and Technological Advances section where we left off."

Doing as Vincent instructed, I saw the computer replace Knowlton with two men and a somewhat more modern-looking computer.

"This is Richard Shoup and Alvy Ray Smith," Vincent explained. "They are credited with developing the first computer paint system, which influenced virtually all paint systems currently in use today."

"Are they still active in the business?" I asked.

Yes, and like many other computer graphics pioneers, Shoup and Smith have gone on to head major computer graphics companies," the computer said. "Shoup founded Aurora Systems, one of the large workstation manufacturers for paint graphics systems. Alvy Ray Smith

went on to become a senior executive at Pixar, one of the leading computer animation programming and production facilities in the world."

"But what are they doing here?" I asked.

"This is the Xerox Palo Alto Research Center, or PARC, in California where Shoup and Smith worked together in the early seventies," Vincent explained. "There, in 1973, Shoup originated the idea for the first interactive animation system and developed the first user-friendly raster display."

"Smith transferred to the New York Institute of Technology Computer Graphics Laboratory at Westbury, Long Island, in 1975," Vincent continued as the hologram setting changed. "NYIT, then as now, was one of the leading centers of computer graphics research, and it was there that Smith produced PAINT."

erpret his ideas to the comput-
" I asked.

didn't happen until the mid- to
e-1970s," Vincent replied, "when
second generation of computer
ists developed. They were differ-
from the early computer artists,
o had to be electronics-knowl-
geable or adept at programming."

hat brought about this change?"
ked.

oftware, mostly. By the late
'0s, computers had become more
cessible and easier to use,"
ncent explained. "With more
phisticated software, computer
sts could simply use the comput-
without having to program it."

I like to know more about some
hose software advances," I said.

I was still trying to understand
how nuclear physics
could possibly relate
to computer graphics.

"That name sounds familiar. Aren't there paint programs on today's computers?"

"Right. PAINT was the prototype for most of the paint systems currently on the market," Vincent replied.

I remembered how I had experimented a bit with the paint program that came with my computer. "Up to this point, it appears that all computer graphics programs were based on math," I said. "But in the paint program I've tried, there was no math involved, at least not on the surface. You could simply draw with it."

"You've picked up on exactly why paint systems became so popular," Vincent said as he demonstrated some techniques on the computer Shoup and Smith had worked on. "The tools were like what artists use in traditional painting techniques. You could paint with a brush and move things across the screen. These paint systems brought the computer to the level where artists were used to working."

"Right," I said.

"In addition to paint systems, Shoup and Smith also developed

frame buffers," Vincent said. "Are you familiar with the term?"

"No," I said.

"I'll explain it then," Vincent said. "A frame buffer is a specific memory device for holding raster graphics. A raster graphic is created from *bitmaps*, a collection of small, separate dots. A vector graphic is created from mathematical formulas for the directional lines, *vectors*, that compose the image. It's also known as an object-oriented graphic. You need to understand the difference between the two to understand frame buffers."

"I think I do."

"As you begin creating art on the computer, you'll more fully grasp the concept," Vincent said. "What you need to know now is that if you put an image into a frame buffer,

you can then paint over the top of it, or change the hue, saturation, and brightness for every dot in it." I watched as Shoup made several adjustments to the image on the screen.

"Now, that I don't quite get," I said.

"Look at it this way," Vincent said. "You're working on an oil painting. If you have nowhere to set your painting and you have no brushes to get to it, then you have no way to work with it.

"What Shoup and Smith did was create a table, a place to put your painting. And with the paint program, you had access to any brush you wanted to paint over the top of it. The frame buffer was simply a memory device where you could load an image, work with it, and when you were done, save it onto your hard drive."

"In the mid to late 1970s, high-end computer graphics research focused on the simulation of light and shading of surfaces."

"So why don't vector graphics need frame buffers?" I asked.

"Vector graphics are created from blocks of code," Vincent explained as the image on the screen became a wireframe model. Smith began manipulating the lines that made up the model. "You can move objects around and do whatever you want with them, but you don't need to a place to set your artwork while you're working on it," Vincent said.

All this technical information was starting to make my head swim. "I'd like to take a break from the technology for a bit," I said. "Could we return to the people section?"

"Sure. And don't worry about trying to absorb everything at once," Vincent assured me. "I won't be giving a pop quiz at the end of the lesson."

"Good." After hitting the ESC key, and clicking *The People of Computer Art*, I scanned the menu of names. Vincent had mentioned Lillian Schwartz earlier, so I clicked her name.

"Lillian Schwartz was an accomplished artist who had been exploring art and technology with her work at contemporary art

shows when she became interested in computer graphics," Vincent explained as a hologram of Lillian Schwartz appeared.

"She joined Bell Labs in the late 1960s, which was the place to go if you wanted to experiment with computer technology."

"But she was an artist first," I said. "She wasn't an engineer who decided to try creating computer art."

"That's right," Vincent replied. "Her goal was to expand the artistic potential for computer graphics. When she got started, it was still dominated by mathematics. But for Schwartz, the computer scientist's algorithms provided a means for turning her traditional artwork into computer-generated images. And her artwork served a useful purpose for the scientists."

"What purpose was that?" I asked.

"For the scientists, her original works of art provided a new source of imagery for their processing techniques. It gave them something new to work with."

"There still was a need to give computer graph-ics a greater feel for art, though" I remarked.

"That's true" Vincent said. "You have to remember, only a limited number of people had access to computer technology at the time. The artists who had access tried very hard to bring together the disparate personalities of art and science."

"It wasn't easy, was it?" I asked, although I felt certain of Vincent's answer.

"No, and the conflict of art and science wasn't the only problem," Vincent explained. "By the end of the 1970s, computer graphics had a new problem: repetitiveness."

"Everybody was doing the same thing," I said.

"Right. At that time, computers w[ere] much more accessible than they [had] been when artists like Lill[ian] Schwartz got involved," Vincent s[aid]. "Unfortunately, only a few progra[ms] and types of equipment were re[adily] available. So naturally, artists co[uld] create a very limited range of ima[ges] and these images were overused."

"Did other traditional artists run [into] similar problems?" I asked.

"Oh, sure," Vincent said as Lil[lian] Schwartz and her art disappea[red]. "Let's meet David Em. He wa[s a] prominent artist in the seventies [who] got interested in computer art, bu[t he] didn't quite know what he wante[d to] do."

"Did he have problems working [with] early computers like other art[ists] did?" I asked.

21

ot at all," Vincent shook his head.
avid Em was a self-proclaimed hack-
You know what a hacker is, don't
u?"

es." Even though I wasn't one, I
w what they were.

od," Vincent said as the computer
ught up a new image. "Now then,
vid had several hacker friends, and
ether they tried doing new things
h computers and technology."

ch as?"

ell, one of their more successful
tures was displaying some of
vid's artwork on a television moni-
," Vincent replied. "But, it was
ough Dick Shoup and Alvy Ray
ith that he found his way in the field
omputer art."

I noticed Shoup and Smith had joined Em in the computer's hologram. "How did they do that?" I asked.

Smith and Shoup were at PARC working on the frame buffer at the time," Vincent explained, "and they invited David to come in and take a look at it, along with Smith's interactive paint program, Superpaint."

The scene shifted to a darkened room, and I could see the three men working with glowing white brush strokes on the computer screen.

"It was January 6, 1975, David Em's first visit to PARC," Vincent said. "Immediately, he knew he had found what he was looking for. Alvy Ray Smith spent the day teaching David how to use the program, and he even programmed in an airbrush right there on the spot.

"This was a watershed event for David Em," Vincent continued. "Now he knew what he wanted to do with computers. The only problem was, even though he had found the tools he

wanted to use, he had trouble getting his hands on them."

"Why was that?" I asked.

"A machine like the one they were using that day in 1975 was pretty much confined to advanced research cen-ters like PARC," Vincent explained. "The programs themselves were still difficult to use, even for people who knew what they were doing. And they kept breaking down, too.

"To top it off, for the art you did create, you had prob-lems with output." Vincent continued, "There just wasn't an easy way to pro-duce hard copies. Many people were creating superb examples of com-puter art, but they had no way to show them."

"So what could you do?" I asked.

"Visual communications are
increasingly important in our society,
and the computer is a marvelous tool for that."

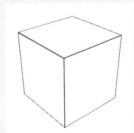

Vincent pointed to the sides of the cube Rober[t] had drawn on the chalkboard. "It would sho[w] both the front and back faces of the cube, an[d] not block out what the human eye couldn['t] see," he said.

Then, Vincent erased the lines creating th[e] back face. "With this algorithm, the compute[r] would see and display 3-D images the same way people see them."

"Now I understand," I said.

"Good," Vincent said as Roberts disappeared. "The next major advancement in 3-D happened simultaneously at MAGI in Elmsfor, New York, and at the University of Utah in the late 1960s. Up to that time, all three-dimensional models were depicted in linear wireframes. On the screen, you could only see the edges of the shapes or objects."

"What was their breakthrough?" I asked.

"Researchers at MAGI devised SynthaVision, a system for modeling solids based on primitive mathematical shapes such as spheres, cubes, and cones that could be rendered directly on the screen. This gave the wireframes a solid surface so you could see them in non-wireframe form. The system could model with constructive solid geometry, in which a complex solid is built out of a simpler solid primitive."

"Well, David Em took a rather unorthodox approach," Vincent said with a touch of irony in his voice. "He went to work for the Jet Propulsion Laboratory in Pasadena, California." The hologram's scene shifted again.

"The lab involved with the space program?" I asked, curious and skeptical at the same time.

"That's the one," Vincent replied. "He joined JPL in the late seventies, where they were constantly pushing the envelope of hardware and software with some of the most advanced computers in the world. Besides working on practical applications for NASA, he basically got to experiment with the system."

After David Em faded away, I decided to go back to the technical advances section. Looking at the menu, I selected three-dimensional art, having always been curious about 3-D images.

"Did the researchers in Utah do something different?" I asked.

"Yes; they developed an alternative solution in which the wireframe models, being in a vector format, could display shaded surfaces with an impression of solidity on a raster screen," Vincent replied. "You remember the difference between raster and vector, don't you?"

I nodded. "Somewhat."

"Basically, this process turned a vector image into a raster image," Vincent continued.

The computer brought up a new hologram, and after revisiting the late sixties and seventies in most of the recent scenes, I was surprised to see a man dressed from at least a decade earlier. Also, unlike some of the more flamboyant artists I had met, he looked decidedly like a scientist.

"This is Lawrence Roberts, one of the pioneers in 3-D graphics," Vincent said. "He was at MIT in 1963, developing an algorithm that would remove those lines that are normally invisible to the human eye."

"What do you mean?" I asked.

"Take a cube for example. It has front faces, and if it's drawn in perspective, it also has back faces," Vincent explained as Roberts drew on a chalkboard behind him. "Until Roberts wrote this algorithm, the computer could not understand the difference between the front and back."

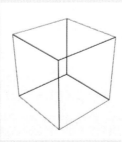

FROM CONCEPT
FROM CONCEPT
FROM CONCEPT
FROM CONCEPT

"How?" I interrupted.

Vincent didn't miss a beat. "By using shading algorithms, a process in which solid objects are modeled by a series of connected polygons. The researchers at Utah also found a way to build a sphere with nothing but flat surface polygons," he smiled slightly. "An unusual approach, wouldn't you say?"

I nodded. "Wouldn't that be impossible?"

"Not at all," Vincent replied, holding out a sphere. "They built a sphere like this by subdividing it into multiple flat surfaces. The more subdivisions you have, the greater the complexity and the smoother the sphere itself. This is the same process necessary to create a 3-D image. One sphere can be made of hundreds of smaller planar facets all connected together." Vincent brought the sphere out where I could look at it close up and see how the flat planes created the smooth surface.

When I was finished examining the sphere, I noticed the scene had changed. Vincent introduced the men in the new hologram as Henri Gouraud and Edwin Catmull, both computer scientists at the University of Utah.

"Gouraud and Catmull took 3-D imaging a step further," Vincent explained. "First, Gouraud perfected a technique that blurred the shading of the facets and gave a polygonal-defined model a smooth appearance."

"So he created an illusion of smoothness where there were sharp edges," I said.

"Right," Vincent replied, holding out a sphere that had been smoothed by Gouraud's algorithm. "Think how you would use wood putty and paint to smooth a joint. Gouraud's algorithm blurred the facets in the connection of the two polygons in the same way."

I didn't bother to tell Vincent that I rarely picked up a hammer, much less smoothed wooden joints, even though I understood his analogy.

"Catmull took a different approach from Gouraud when it came to rendering modeled objects," Vincent said. "He defined surfaces directly as curves in space rather than a series of facets. That way, he didn't have to use polygons to create spheres." Vincent held out another sample.

"It looks a bit more realistic, doesn't it?" I asked.

"I think so," Vincent said. "But for even more realistic images, you had to use a technique known as *ray tracing*." Gouraud and Catmull had disappeared.

"What's that?"

"I'll explain in a minute," Vincent replied. "You should know that as computers became more powerful, the graphics they produced became more sophisticated as well. So, many people in the field began pursuing more realistic images."

"And ray tracing was the way to do it?" I asked.

"Quite by accident, yes," Vincent said. "Ray tracing is the most successful technique for defining light on the computer, but it wasn't originally developed for computer graphics."

"What was it developed for then?"

Vincent gave me a deadpan look. "Nuclear radiation shielding," he said.

"You've got to be kidding."

"Honest," Vincent was clearly amused by my skepticism. "Phillip Mittelman, a nuclear physicist at MAGI, was working to develop nuclear radiation shielding when he developed this process in the late 1960s. Turner Whitted then expanded on Mittelman's research at the University of North Carolina at Chapel Hill."

I couldn't begin to understand how nuclear physics would relate to computer graphics. "Can you explain it?" I asked.

"Sure," Vincent replied. "Ray tracing is an extremely complex process. It consists of an algorithm that traces hypothetical beams of light from the viewer's point of

"The computer has become the standard graphic design tool in advertising and the production of printed artwork and graphics."

vision back to the light source. Each pixel in the display is regarded as multiple rays."

"Wouldn't that require a lot of rays?" I asked. "Especially considering all the pixels needed to create an image."

"You're absolutely right," Vincent said. "It takes more than a million rays to compute a high-resolution image. Ray tracing is so computationally intensive that it takes a computer with a lot of horsepower. It's also very expensive, even today."

"So it isn't used extensively," I said.

"Unfortunately, no. Because of its complexity and high cost, it really has to be used sparingly. But when ray tracing is employed," Vincent said, holding up a beautifully detailed drawing, "the effect is stunning."

"It sure looks real," was all I could say.

After Whitted was gone, I called up the menu and scanned the choices, finally clicking on the Shading and Texture section. The computer brought up the images of two men who Vincent introduced as Bui-Tuong Phong and James Blinn.

"In the mid to late 1970s, high-end computer graphics research focused on the simulation of light and shading of surfaces," Vincent explained. "In 1975, Bui-Tuong Phong created a lighting model that provided the effect of realistic illumination from a direct light source."

"How did he do that?" I asked, a question that had now become almost automatic.

"There were a couple of ways," Vincent replied. "But the most effective way was to create a highlight on the surface of an object when it was lit. The effect was highly realistic."

"What about texture?" I asked.

"That was Blinn's development," Vincent replied. "He defined a set of algorithms for bump mapping while a doctoral candidate at Utah in 1976."

"And bump mapping created texture?" I asked.

"Actually, bump mapping created an *illusion* of surface texture," Vincent explained, holding out a couple of illustrations. "Some of his early experiments using strawberries and oranges did look fairly convincing, don't you think?"

Even upon close examination, the bump-mapping samples had a realistic quality. "So what did Blinn do after he got his doctorate?" I asked.

"He went to work at JPL, just like David Em," Vincent said. "There, he developed some advanced graphics and animation software, and created convincing simulations of the Voyager I spacecraft during its visit to Jupiter in 1979."

"I remember those!" I exclaimed. "Voyager sent back all those stunning images."

"And Blinn created the simulations that accompanied the pictures from space," Vincent said as the computer brought up one of Blinn's simulations. "Remember this one showing Jupiter as it appeared to Voyager I?"

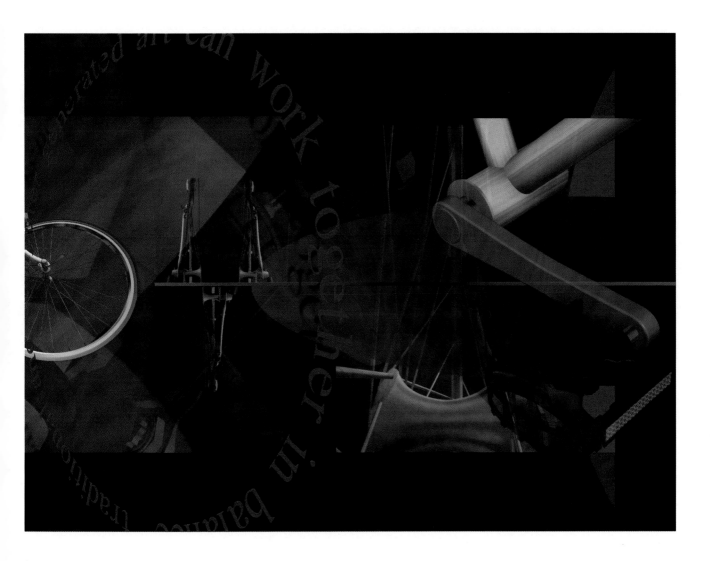

I nodded. "Those swirling clouds looked so real."

"The Jupiter fly-bys astonished the computer graphics community as well as the public at large," Vincent said. "This was one of the first times computer animation had such widespread exposure."

"I never knew those were computer generated," I said as Jupiter, Blinn, and Phong faded away. "Amazing."

Returning to planet Earth, I hit the ESC key and clicked Film and Animation, the only remaining section in the Events and Technological Advances menu.

"This section introduces you to several people," Vincent explained, "and you'll also revisit a couple of artists you've already met." He introduced the first person the computer brought up as Edward Zajec, another scientist at Bell Labs.

"It seems that a lot of technological breakthroughs came out of Bell Labs," I observed.

"Bell Labs was one of the major institutions for computer graphics research — and it still is," Vincent said. "But there were others such as the IBM Thomas J. Watson Research Center, the Los Alamos National Laboratory in New Mexico, the Lawrence Livermore National Laboratory in California, and, as you've seen, the Jet Propulsion Laboratory."

"Right," I nodded.

"Anyway," Vincent continued, "Zajec's contribution to computer graphics was the first computer-generated film, produced in 1963. That same year saw the introduction of the microfilm recorder."

"So now you had a way to record images." I noted.

Vincent nodded. "Zajec realized early on that computer graphics could be a valuable resource in communicating ideas," he said. "So when Zajec was working on a theory to determine whether a satellite in space could be stabilized so that one of its sides was constantly facing the earth, he thought computer animation was a logical way to present his findings."

"And was it?" I asked.

"See for yourself," Vincent said as the computer brought up Zajec's animation. The satellite pitched and yawed for a few seconds, then pointed steadily as is went around a sphere representing Earth."

"Thanks to Zajec's pioneering work, computer animation is now used all the time to illustrate complex ideas."

The computer then brought up another hologram. "This is Nam June Paik, and he developed some of the first computer enhancements of video images to create animations and special video effects," Vincent said. "The Paik-Abe video synthesizer that he developed could distort, reshape, re-color or colorize video images."

"All those techniques are still common today, aren't they?" I asked.

"Oh sure; he's still active in the field," Vincent replied as Paik's image was replaced by a new one. "This is Stanley Van Der Beek, another Bell Labs alumnus."

"Was he a computer scientist or an artist?" I asked, knowing that both types of people seemed to thrive there.

"More of an artist, I'd say," Vincent replied. "Before he got involved with computers, he was an experimental film maker. Early on, he realized that computers could be used for artistic purposes in the field of animation and video. Together with Mike Noll, he worked on the first computer animation at Bell Labs back in 1964. It was a project dedicated exclusively to aesthetic purposes."

Lillian Schwartz and Kenneth Knowlton then joined the hologram. "Lillian Schwartz also did some animation at Bell Labs," Vincent said. "With Kenneth Knowlton's help, they animated some of her still graphics." He held up an image. "One of the most famous of these was Pixillation, produced in 1970."

The Bell Labs group faded away as Charles Csuri appeared in a new image. "I thought you already explained his involvement in computer animation," I said. "Didn't he develop the animation software that IBM demonstrated in their showroom?"

"Right," Vincent said. "But also in 1970, he established the Computer Graphics Research Group at Ohio State to continue advancing computer animation research."

"What kind of advancements?" I asked.

"Well, one of the major ones came early," Vincent replied. "In 1971, graduate student Tom DeFanti developed GRASS, which stood for Graphics Symbiosis System. It was the first easily programmable animation language.

"The group also earned acclaim for its work in the modeling of human motion," Vincent continued. "People could use the computer to choreograph a pattern of motion and see it immediately on the screen."

"Was their choreography accurate?" I asked.

"Gradually it became more so," Vincent replied. "Their work brought new attention to the need to create photo-realism and human-based art. Early computer animators wanted to accurately re-create human motion, and this spilled over into still imagery as well."

"It's the same with traditional art," I remarked. "Of course, you already know that."

Vincent smiled. "I think when you explore some of the theory section you'll understand even more," he said. "And now that you've completed the technological achievements and people sections of the program, that's all we have left to cover."

"So these are the people and events that made computer graphics what it is today," I said.

Vincent hesitated. "Well, this program cannot cover *everything*," he hedged. "But now you know the highlights."

"In other words, I've seen the who, what, when, where, and how," I said. "Now it's time for the why."

"Exactly," Vincent replied. "*Computer Art Techniques and Theories* is basically one big section. The ideas we'll be discussing tend to flow from one to the next.

"Now, you probably already know what I'm about to tell you," he continued, "but a fundamental concept of art is that it's more than just a finished visual that you can hang on the wall. it's a process of experimenting and exploring new approaches, testing ideas."

"I do know that," I pointed out. "I experiment a lot in my work. And that's one reason why I'm thinking about computer art — to explore."

"I'm just trying to cover all the bases, Vincent said. "I'm glad you're open to experimentation; that was one of the things that EAT did very well.

"As you probably know," he continued, "art comes from the eagerness to challenge different perspectives and the way we view different things. The computer has served as a powerful tool with which an artist can experiment."

"Art is always evolving, too," I remarked.

"And that will continue as comput themselves evolve," Vincent continu "Computer artists of the future will taking ideas where they've never g before.

"But, back to practicality," Vincent c tinued. "Quite frankly, computers m a superb artist's tool because they sent great opportunities to expl ideas and approaches. Computers c powerful tools that let us create id more quickly than any other way."

"The faster you can produce so thing, and the more you can prod the more you can sell," I ackno

31

VisionEtics

jed. "I love art, but I do have to sup-
t myself."

osolutely," Vincent nodded. "But
n for the amateur, they provide an
let for those who wish to simply
ate art." He paused. "You've hit on
ood point. Of course, being an artist
tainly isn't the fastest or easiest way
et rich."

n not a millionaire yet," I said,
ghing.

cent smiled broadly. "Well, that's
y. If it was easy to get rich as an

artist, there would be too many artists
and not enough good art. Still, as you
know, it's possible to support yourself
as an artist, and there are several areas
in computer graphics that are growing
and will need more good artists as the
computer's capabilities continue to
grow. Now, you're basically a traditional artist who's just beginning to explore
computer graphics, right?"

"Yes."

"Well then," Vincent said. "You probably aren't aware of some of the oppor-

tunities where you can
expand your talents and, to
be totally crass, make
some money."

"I'm open," I said.

"One of the most explo-
sive growth areas will be
in education, training, and
marketing software,"
Vincent continued. "It's
becoming more common
as computers grow more
powerful. Visual com-
munications are increas-
ingly important in our
society, and the com-
puter is a marvelous
tool for that."

"Which this program
has already proven," I
remarked.

"You bet," Vincent
agreed. "But of
course, computers
can't create images

**"One of the most
explosive growth areas will be
in education, training,
and marketing software."**

spontaneously. That's why there will be a great need for artists to create the visual communication elements of future computers. Whether these images are rendered by hand or by the computers, it still requires an artist to determine how the system might flow — that's an art form unto itself — as well as how the human/computer interface will look. You'll never be able to replace the human element in computer graphics," he said with confidence.

"I would think the entertainment industry will continue to be a hot market for computer graphics," I observed. "Look at all the special effects they can create with computers."

"Right, but what's really great is that up until recently, most of the special effects and other fun things that the entertainment industry gets to do has involved very sophisticated, complex — and therefore, extremely expensive — computers," Vincent said. "This kind of technology has been out of reach for most desktop computer artists like you.

"But," he said, with a gleam in his eye, "that's changing. You've seen it happen as computer technology gradually trickles down to where more people can use it. As computers and software become more powerful, yet more accessible to a wider audience, more computer artists will be able to perform video editing and create special effects — just like in the movies — on their desktop computers. It's already beginning to happen."

"I guess you could call it the democratization of the computer — giving more of its power to the people," I said.

Vincent nodded. "It has and will continue to have an incredible effect on the creative artist community," he said. "The computer serves as an outlet for people with creative minds to see their ideas come to life. With greater access to the video, animation, and art equipment previously available only to big-budget productions, more artists will be able to produce effects on a level with big-budget studios. We'll see an onslaught of all types of imagery and new creativity by giving more people access to powerful artistic tools."

"Hasn't that already happened with desktop publishing?" I asked. "That's sort of what sparked my interest in computer graphics."

"Definitely. The computer has become the standard graphic design tool in advertising and the production of printed artwork and graphics," Vincent said. "A lot of people involved with computer graphics predicted this kind of thing would happen early on."

"It's almost become essential," I noted. "You'd have to be in the stone age not to take advantage of the computer for producing printed artwork."

"Computers now have the capability to readily process high-color and high-resolution imagery, as well as scan and manipulate images," Vincent said. "For the print production artist, the computer has become an all-encompassing, highly versatile tool. Many of today's magazines, books, advertisements, and other print media are produced entirely by computer. None of the pre-printing work is done by hand."

"I'll bet that trend will continue," I said. "Eventually, the entire printing process could be done in digital form."

Vincent nodded. "Computers will never replace the talents of the artist, but they have replaced many of the traditional methods used to produce artwork." He paused. "This isn't necessarily good or bad; there are still instances where it makes sense to create art the old-fashioned way. But, that won't stop the evolution toward creating art digitally."

"Computers have certainly changed our lives," I noted.

"For the better mostly," Vincent said. "A funny thing happened along the way, though."

"You'll never be able to replace the human element in computer graphics."

"What's that?" I asked, immediately curious.

"Well, when computers were invented, one of the things we had hoped for and envisioned was a paperless society."

"That hasn't happened," I said.

"Not at all. Since the advent of computers, we've used even more paper."

"Well, that's easy to explain," I said. "You do something with the computer. Then you have to print a copy so you can take a look at it."

Vincent picked up the thought. "Of course, you have to make some changes. Then you print another copy to look over the changes."

By now, I was laughing at the absurdity of the situation. "And so on and so on."

Vincent looked amused. "Well, we'll break the pattern eventually," he said. "More and more, information will be delivered in an electronic format to our homes and desktops. Modems, electronic mail, and other mediums are already accomplishing this. But we will continue to need better information faster, and one of the best ways to do this is via the computer."

"I know the computer is already used extensively to produce audiovisual presentations as well as corporate reports and presenta-

tions," I said. "It's an area I'd like to explore in my business."

"The computer's ever-expanding role in art, entertainment, business, and everyday life gives you more opportunities to work and grow artistically," Vincent said.

"That's good news for me," I noted.

"People and businesses are going to need to maintain many communications networks," Vincent continued. "And computer artists will be needed to create the interfaces and produce the images that

everyday computer users can work with. As a society, we're approaching information overload, so it will be part of the computer artist's job to help us manage all that information."

"It sounds like I have an exciting future ahead," I said.

"You do," Vincent replied. "And I think you have the right perspective about computers. As I've said, there are many areas where computer art will continue to grow, but bottom line, it is the artist, not the com-

"Of course," Vincent replied. "And for some of those people with traditional art backgrounds, such as Lillian Schwartz, computer art is a medium that can very well change the creative process for a person."

"Well, art is the process of experimenting with ideas," I said.

"When you get down to basics," Vincent said, "the creative process is where experimentation brings to light new ideas and new forms of art. If it takes less time for that experimentation to occur, and you can see the results of that experimentation more quickly, that changes the creative process. Computers have done that."

He paused, looking serious. "It also poses a new problem."

"What's that?"

"One of the most difficult lessons for people to learn — and one that many aspiring computer artists struggle with — is knowing how to handle the power that comes from the computer," he said seriously. "The danger lies in having your creative agendas sidetracked by the lure of astonishing technical feats."

"I think I know what you mean," I said. "If you sit down at the computer with an idea, your mind could just go wild knowing how the computer lifts many limitations."

"Right," Vincent said. "You go off on these tangents because you want to explore all kinds of different creative options. Your original intentions could be thoroughly sidetracked. This can be good because it furthers the creative process, so long as you've aware of the computer's power for sparking your creativity."

"You could end up with something completely different from what you planned to produce," I remarked.

Vincent looked thoughtful. "That's not necessarily bad, but you do need to have a specific goal in mind when you begin to create art on the computer," he said. "You also have to learn patience. The early computer artists certainly did."

"Well, computers back then were awfully complex and hard to work with," I remarked.

"Oh, they're still complex," Vincent said warily. "In many ways, today's computers are much more complex than the ones from the sixties and seventies. You're just shielded somewhat from that complexity by, quote, user-friendly software, unquote.

ter, who will make computer art ppen. Computer hardware and ftware will become more powerful cause of the people developing m. And the field of computer art l go where and as far as the peo- involved take it."

he people you've introduced me oday can certainly point to some redible achievements, " I noted.

"One of the most difficult

lessons for people

to learn is knowing how to handle

the power that comes from the computer."

"But probably the most important lesson you can learn," Vincent continued, "is to understand that the computer is simply a tool. It doesn't necessarily have to be the final means of producing something. There is a temptation to use the computer exclusively, but it is not always the best tool for you to use."

"That makes sense," I said. "but I'd like to hear why."

"Well then," Vincent said, "say you're used to creating art with watercolors or pastels. With media like these, the act of randomness and the forces of nature create something that looks completely different from what a lot of computer artwork looks like."

"So where is the problem?" I asked.

"Well, there is the temptation — and it happens among both professional and amateur artists — to do all your work on the computer, simply because you can."

"To play the devil's advocate," I said, "why shouldn't you?"

"It's simple," Vincent replied. "If you want to create something that looks like it was done with a watercolor brush, then that's what you should use. Despite all its capabilities, a computer still cannot quite achieve the same effect."

"Of course, somebody may eventually write a program that effectively recreates all the forces of nature that might come into play in doing a watercolor brush stroke," I countered.

"You're probably right," he acknowledged. "But even so, it will never be as true as the actual thing. The lesson is that you should use a watercolor brush stroke if that's the effect you want to create. Then, bring it into the computer and let the computer augment the artwork. Remember this: there's no need to waste your time trying to get the computer to reproduce what you can do more effectively using traditional methods."

"In other words, traditional and computer generated art can work together in balance," I said.

"Absolutely," Vincent replied. "You just have to keep it all in perspective. If you do that, I think you have the potential to be a great computer artist," he said.

Even though Vincent was just a computer hologram, his compliment still made me feel good. "Thanks for

explaining it all to me, Vincent," I said. "I think this afternoon may have changed my life."

"Well, good," he said with a firm nod of his head. "Just remember to call on me anytime when you start experimenting with computer graphics."

"I'll do that," I promised. "I think I'm going to need some of your expertise."

Vincent grinned as his image began to fade. "You're probably right. Keep experimenting, keep exploring. Who knows, maybe you'll join the people you've met today in the history of great computer artists."

"I certainly hope so," I said thoughtfully as he was gone.

Epilogue

After Vincent faded completely, I returned to the main menu. I could see through the broken windows that the sun was going down. It was time to leave, so, reluctantly, I quit the program and shut down the computer.

The lock to the door I had come in still worked. I locked and closed the door firmly behind me — even though anybody who really wanted to could easily break it down — and walked to my car.

I noticed with some relief that it hadn't been stripped or stolen. Now I had to find the nearest pay phone, I thought as I drove off.

Fortunately, there was a convenience store only a couple of blocks away. I fumbled through my address book, dug out a quarter, and called my real estate agent's office.

"I'm awfully sorry" the receptionist said in his most apologetic tone. "Dave got called away at the very last minute. We tried to reach you, but I guess you had already left to meet him. Would you like to try looking at the property tomorrow at 2:00?"

"No, that's all right," I said, my voice barely able to contain my excitement over the treasure I had found. "Just tell Dave I'll take it."

"If you want to create something that looks like it was done with a watercolor brush, then that's what you should use."

2 Underst

How
Computers

I now owned that old warehouse.

Dave, my real estate agent, though somewhat surprised by my message, started the miles of paperwork necessary to complete the sale, but for all intents and purposes, it was mine.

And so was the computer I had found there. I casually mentioned it to Dave, who said it was probably abandoned, didn't work, and I was welcome to whatever scrap value it or its parts had. I didn't tell him just how well it worked.

Nor did I tell anybody else. I really wasn't sure myself what had happened that afternoon in the warehouse. I did know, however, that I definitely wanted to learn more about computer art.

I did tell a few friends and other artists that I was going to explore computer

anding

Work

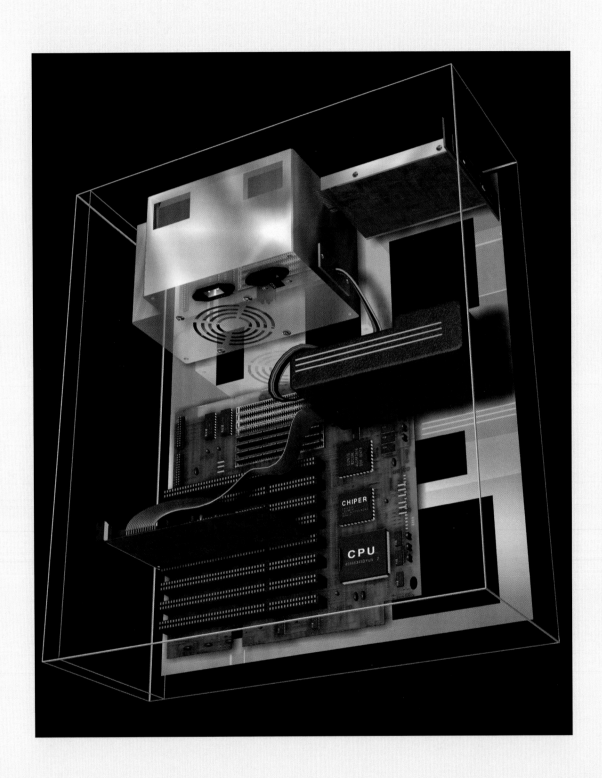

graphics in my new studio, which came as surprise to them. The general consensus was, "What do you know about computer art? You barely know how to turn on a computer, much less how to produce computer graphics."

Much as I hated to admit it, they were right. An afternoon of exposure to the history of computer graphics had certainly caught my attention, but I really needed to know more about how computers worked before I could reasonably expect to create art with one. After all, I reasoned, it was the same as using any other artist's tool, although figuring out how brushes work didn't seem nearly as complicated.

So I went back to the warehouse. I had put a sturdier door and lock on the place almost immediately, and going inside, I found the computer was still there.

When I turned on the computer this time, it went through the normal startup routine, then nothing, just a blinking cursor on the screen. No holograms came up. No Vincent.

Not exactly sure what to do, I typed "Vincent, are you in there?"

No response.

"Hello," I typed.

Still no response.

It was time for a shot in the dark. "Vincent, where are you?" I called, feeling absolutely ridiculous to be yelling at an inanimate object.

But it appeared to work. After a few seconds, the computer began to whir, then finally, the monitor cranked up and a hologram of Vincent appeared. He smiled broadly.

"You're back!" Vincent said cheerfully. "You must be taking me up on the offer to learn more."

"Yes," I replied. "I've bought this building to use as my new studio."

Vincent nodded approvingly. "It is a bit run down," he noted, "but there's definitely potential here. Lots of open space; I like that."

"I want to learn more about how computers work," I told him. "I think it will make me a better computer artist."

"It can't hurt," Vincent agreed.

"Can you help me?" I asked.

"Well, of course, that's why I'm here," Vincent said. "In fact, I'll take you on an inside tour of the computer?"

I looked skeptically at the machine in front of me. "Somehow, I don't think I'd fit through the disk drive," I said.

Vincent laughed. "You don't go inside; the computer projects its inner working into a hologram," he said. "Just like it projects me."

"That'll work."

"Good," Vincent said as the computer brought up a new hologram, "We're going to start off by looking at a computer from the early days." The hologram was complete now, a big hulking monster of a machine.

"The first computers took up entire rooms," Vincent continued. "They consisted primarily of vacuum tubes, which functioned as electronic switches."

"I want to learn more about how computers work," I told him. "I think it will make me a better computer artist."

"Switches?" I wasn't what you'd call mechanically competent.

"Yes," Vincent replied. "That's all a computer is when you boil it down; it's a collection of on/off switches."

"It can't be that simple, can it?" I was really skeptical now.

"At its most basic level, yes," Vincent replied. "By turning on a series of those switches, you can create a pattern, like signs that spell out letters with light bulbs. The computer can also sense which switches are on or off, and based on that information, turn more switches on or off. It's part of the binary code that all computers operate under."

"What's the binary code?" I asked.

"For the computer, everything is either a 1 or a 0, which corresponds to on and off," Vincent replied. "These are known as bits, and from the 1 and 0, the computer can create any number or letter."

"Amazing how the computer breaks everything down into something so simple," I remarked.

Vincent turned his attention back to the huge old computer and its collection of vacuum tubes. "These vacuum tubes created a lot of heat," he said, wiping sweat from his forehead, "which caused components to fail and made early computers famous for frequent breakdowns. They also consumed enormous amounts of electricity."

"Then how was the problem solved?" I asked. "Aren't we still using vacuum tubes?"

"Not exactly," Vincent replied. "Computers nowadays use transistors, which are essentially vacuum tubes on a microscopic scale."

"Those big tubes could shrink that much?"

"Oh sure," Vincent replied. "A typical microprocessor chip contains more than a million transistors. Going from vacuum tubes to transistors dramatically shrank the amount of space a computer required — which is why a computer that once took up an entire room can now fit on your lap. Transistors also use less power and generate a lot less heat. That made computers virtually one hundred percent reliable."

"Do all chips have that many transistors?" I asked.

"It varies," Vincent replied. "Transistors are arranged on the chip in different patterns so that they can do different things. Manufacturers are experimenting with X-rays to fit even more transistors on a single chip. Eventually, transistors might get down to the molecular level, where the presence or absence of just one electron could signal the on/off state."

"Amazing," I said. "Well, now, can you explain how a transistor works?"

"Sure, that's easy."

With that, the hologram changed again. At first, it appeared to be a normal computer blown up to giant size. Then, it was as though Vincent was taking me inside the computer as the view zoomed through the floppy disk drive, past circuit boards and cables, then under one of the larger chips.

"This," Vincent said, pointing to the chip we had just been under, "is a microprocessor chip, which is also known as the central processing unit or CPU."

"This chip contains more than a million transistors, and more than a thousand transistors can fit on a single slice of silicon," Vincent said. "The silicon is then embedded in plastic and attached to metal leads that connect the transistors to other parts of the computer circuit. Leads carry signals to and from the chip to other components inside the computer."

"And the transistor processes those signals?" I asked.

"Right," Vincent replied. "In basic terms, a transistor acts as a valve that permits the control of a larger voltage. A positive charge turns the transistor on, which represents a 1."

"And a negative charge?"

That turns the transistor off, representing 0," Vincent replied.

The image of the hologram now zoomed back out from under the chip to show it and several other parts of the computer.

"This," Vincent said, pointing to the chip we had just been under, "is a microprocessor chip, which is also known as the central processing unit or CPU. It serves as the brains of a computer and consists of many different transistors connected together. Those transistors form units, each of which have distinct functions, just like your brain."

"What kind of functions?"

"Well, some units of the CPU obtain data and instructions from memory; some store data and instructions where they can be readily accessed, some make sense of the instructions and carry them out, while others deliver the results back to memory," Vincent said. "And the microprocessor can do all of these tasks simultaneously."

"Does the microprocessor store the data?" I asked.

"No, that's the job of disk storage and random access memory, more commonly known as RAM," Vincent said.

The hologram image of the computer's interior shifted to several, spinning disks with mechanical arms moving back and forth across them. "This is your hard disk," Vincent

explained, "and this is where most of your data gets stored. Think of it as a file cabinet for the central processing unit. Information is stored here until it is needed by the CPU, then filed away again when it's no longer needed."

"How does disk storage work?" I asked.

"Basically, it's a magnetic process," Vincent explained. "An electric charge in the read/write head creates a magnetic field that causes iron particles on the disk to line up as either positive or negative. The computer can then read this information as a 0 or 1."

"What about floppy disks?" I asked.

"The process is the same," Vincent replied. "Floppies don't store as much information and they're slower than hard disks, but they're portable. Now then, let's talk about RAM."

"How is RAM different from your hard drive?" I asked.

"RAM is an electronic version of the hard drive, and information stored in RAM is lost when you turn off your computer," Vincent explained. "It's not magnetic like the hard drive."

"RAM is an electronic version of the hard drive, and information stored in RAM is lost when you turn off your computer."

"Why do you need an electronic version?" I reasoned. "Doesn't the hard drive have enough room to store data?"

"Well, RAM serves a different purpose," Vincent explained. "It's a temporary storage place for information you regularly access while using the computer. And for that purpose, it is better than physically storing data on the hard drive."

"You know I'm going to ask the question," I told Vincent. "Why?"

Vincent was unflappable. "Information can be read almost instantaneously from RAM," he said. "It's a very quick process because there's no coil or mechanism that has to go across a spinning disk to pick up the information."

"Then how do you read and write information to RAM?"

"It's similar to the transistor in the central processing unit," Vincent explained, as the computer brought up a new hologram, a grid where several sections appeared unconnected. "Infor-mation going to RAM sends electronic pulses down this strand of conductive material, which is known as an address line. There are lots of these address lines in a RAM chip."

Along the address line are memory locations where RAM data can be stored," Vincent continued. "Here, the electrical charge closes a circuit with a transistor, turning it on." He pointed to spots where the grid lines were now connected.

"When the transistors are on, the computer sends another electrical pulse down selected data lines," Vincent said, pointing to lines running perpendicular to the address lines. "Each of these pulses is a bit, which stands for either a 1 or a 0."

"Back to the binary code," I remarked.

"Exactly. When that electrical charge reaches one of the tran-sistors that has been turned on along an address line, it flows through the closed transistor and charges a capacitor," Vincent continued. "Data stored in RAM is lost when you turn off the computer because there's no electricity to charge the capacitors.

"To retrieve data stored in RAM, the computer sends another electrical charge down the address line," Vincent continued.

"This again closes the connected transistors.

"The capacitors that have been holding a charge then discharge through the circuit that has been created by the closed transistors. These pulses flow down the data lines. The computer can recognize which data lines are sending a charge, interpreting that charge as a 1. Data lines that don't send a charge are read as 0s. When you string a series of 1s and 0s together from eight data lines, they form letters and numbers, etc."

"But if it takes a whole series of 1s and 0s to form one letter, wouldn't it require an awful lot of RAM memory? How much RAM does a computer need?"

"That varies by computer," Vincent replied. "Most desktop machines have a least two to four megabytes of RAM, but others may have much more. Remember, a megabyte is roughly one million bytes, so that's a lot of data that can be stored."

"You never mentioned bytes before. Is that the same as a bit?" I asked.

"Not quite. A byte consists of eight contiguous bits," Vincent explained. "For example, the binary code for the letter A is 01000001. Each 1 or 0 represents a bit, which in a series of eight bits represents a byte. So a byte, as you can see, is the basic equivalent of one character."

"But if you're working with a long or complex file on the computer, wouldn't it be possible to use up all the RAM?" I asked.

"Absolutely," Vincent said. "All computer programs require a certain amount of RAM to operate because they have to be able to archive and retrieve information the CPU might need to access. The more RAM you have, the more information the program can use at a given time."

"But what happens when you run out of RAM?" I persisted.

"I'll give you an example," Vincent said. "Say you're working in a big graphics program where you're manipulating a 20MB image. If you have just 8MB of RAM, that's going to use up all the information the RAM can hold."

I nodded in understanding.

"If you do something to the image that creates 15MB of information that needs to be manipulated, the CPU is going to use the 8MB it has in RAM, and for the rest, it will create a swap disk or a swap file on the hard drive itself. This is also known as virtual memory."

"What does that mean?" I asked.

"The CPU will grab an open section of the hard drive and use it as a portion of the RAM. Data is then swapped back and forth between the hard drive and RAM. The CPU will ship information to the hard disk in this fake section of RAM and use the actual RAM also."

"How well does this work?" I asked.

"The process itself works just fine; it's simply using the hard disk to make up for the lack of RAM," Vincent explained. "The only problem is, it slows things down. Remember, RAM is an entirely electrical process, which is a lot faster than mechanical storage on the hard drive."

"Remember, a megabyte is roughly one million bytes, so that's a lot of data that can be stored."

"So if you're working with large programs and files, it makes sense to have plenty of RAM on your computer," I remarked.

"You've got it," Vincent nodded approvingly. "Adding RAM to your computer is simple and not terribly expensive in most cases."

"You may want to add other capabilities to your computer as well," Vincent continued as a new hologram brought up an overview of the computer's interior, "which is where expansion slots come in." He pointed to two circuit boards mounted on their sides and two empty slots next to them.

"Expansion slots are plug-in connectors that allow you to insert additional circuit boards, also known as expansion cards, like those two there," Vincent explained. "They attach to the rest of the computer through circuitry known as the bus."

"What kind of things would be added on an expansion card?" I asked.

"All kinds," Vincent said. "There are devices for input and output, faxes, modems, display cards to increase the resolution of your screen, faster processors, the works. Think of expansion slots as a blank canvas where you can customize the computer to fit how you use it."

"I never knew I had that option," I said.

"Well, computers are used in so many ways, they have to be flexible," Vincent explained as he pointed to a flat circuit board with several devices attached. "This is the motherboard," he said. "It holds all the computer's critical components."

I pointed to the large chip mounted on the motherboard. "Isn't that the CPU chip we looked at earlier?" I asked.

"Right you are," Vincent replied. "The CPU, RAM, expansion slots, and interconnecting circuitry are all on or attached to the motherboard."

"You mentioned how the expansion cards were connected to the PC by a bus," I pointed out. "Obviously, a bus in computer terms isn't the same as what you see on the road."

"That's right. The bus is actually a highway where data travels between the expansion slots, RAM, and the CPU," Vincent explained. "The more information that can travel on the bus, the speedier the transmission of information."

"How much data can fit on the bus at one time?" I asked.

"It varies by computer," Vincent replied. "Some older computers have an 8-bit bus, which means only 8 parallel lines of data can be transmitted at one time. Newer computers have 16- or 32-bit buses. On a 16-bit bus, 8 or 16 parallel lines can be transmitted, depending on the adapter card. A 32-bit bus transmits data in 32 parallel lines. This, of course, speeds the amount of information the computer can deal with."

"Okay," I said. "What's next?"

"Let's talk about the monitor," Vincent replied as the hologram shifted again. "I've been telling you how in the computer everything gets boiled down to a 1 or a 0. That's not what you see on the screen because the computer converts the binary code into an alphanumeric system. This way, when you type an *A* on the keyboard, you see an *A*, not *01000001.*"

"That sounds like a pretty straightforward process," I remarked. "But isn't displaying a graphic on the screen a lot more complex?"

"Oh, definitely," Vincent nodded. "Displaying graphics involves bit-depth level, resolution, aspect ratios, and so forth. Color's the big issue, though."

"Why is that?"

"Well, computers display information in what's known as RGB format," Vincent explained. "RGB stands for red, green, and blue, the combination of which creates the colors on your screen, just as with a color TV."

"What's the problem, then?" I asked.

"Well, it mainly affects computer artists and desktop publishers," Vincent replied. "RGB provides a much broader color spectrum than the color process used in printing."

"CMYK," I interrupted.

"Right," Vincent said. "The colors in CMYK — cyan, magenta, yellow, and black — have a color spectrum that's about half of what can be created with RGB."

"So, how do you resolve the problem?"

"Basically, you fudge a little," Vincent said. "You take the information on the computer screen in RGB and match it as closely as possible to the CMYK process. The key words here are *match as closely as possible* because there is

no way to do it to the nth degree — not yet anyway."

"That's to be expected since they're two different processes," I observed.

"True; it's just something computer artists have to be aware of when outputting their color images," Vincent noted.

It appeared to me we had toured all the parts of the computer, yet I still felt something was missing. "Vincent," I said, "you've done a great job of explaining how all the computer's parts work, but it seems there has to be something to make them all work together."

"That's where software comes in," Vincent replied. "Software is basically computer-readable code that allows you to do things. There are two kinds of software. Application software includes word processors, spreadsheets, drawing programs, graphics, and things like that. The other type of software is the operating system, which serves as the link between your applications and the computer's hardware."

"So your applications have to go through the operating system?" I asked.

Vincent nodded. "Operating systems were originally set up to handle the input and output operations the computer would carry out, specifically communicating with

disk drives," he explained. "It evolved into this all-encompassing link because otherwise, every time somebody wrote a piece of software, they'd have to re-create the way the computer would display information on the screen, how it would deal with printers, reading and writing files to disks, and that sort of thing."

"In other words, you'd have to do everything from scratch," I said.

"Right," Vincent agreed. "The operating systems provide a common platform for all the software to work through to complete their jobs.

common platform makes it easier to use."

"I guess that makes sense," I conceded. "I never knew there was so much to learn about how computers work."

"Oh, there's plenty more," Vincent said. "We could spend a few days, maybe weeks...."

"No, that's okay," I interrupted him. "I'm not trying to become a computer engineer or anything." My mind was approaching over-load by now.

"I understand," Vincent smiled. "You know the basics, and that's all you really need right now. But if you ever need help, or just somebody to explain something for you, I'll be around."

"I'll remember that," I said, glad to know help was readily available — and it didn't involve waiting on hold listening to canned music.

His task complete, Vincent began to fade. "Call on me again — anytime," he said as he waved good-bye.

I waved back. "Count on it," I said to the rapidly disappearing hologram.

Again, it was time to leave. It seemed as if I couldn't come to the warehouse without spending the whole afternoon. But in a few weeks, I'd be moving in my studio, and I could spend all the time I wanted to explore computer art. And now that I had a basic idea of how computers worked, I was ready.

"Look at it this way," he continued. "Imagine you were planning a trip somewhere. If the trip is planned out for you, and you know exactly the distances and the exact routes to take, you'll get there a lot faster."

"But isn't it limiting having every-thing mapped out for you?" I asked.

"Well, using the trip analogy, yes," Vincent replied. "Even if you know there's a quicker way to get to your destination, you can't use it be-cause the pre-planned trip that has been set for you. But when you're dealing with software, having a

learning the **fundam** of COMPUTER

chapter 3

I wasn't able to return to Vincent or the computer for a few weeks. Completing my purchase of the warehouse, cleaning it out, fixing it up, and moving my studio in consumed all my time.

Gradually, I transformed the place. The main room in the building became exhibit space for my work, as well as a conference area. There were two large offices in the loft, one of which I used for storage and the copier. The other office was for me.

It was this office, with its bright skylights, where I would do most of my work. I set up my drawing table and all my assorted artist supplies, then very carefully moved the computer I had found from the main room. I needed Vincent, who had become my computer art mentor, handy as I began working.

Now the computer screen was just like a blank canvas, made more daunting by its seemingly limitless capabilities.

A trip to the software store didn't help. There were so many choices: raster, vector, two-dimensional, three-dimensional. Even though Vincent had taken me through the history of computer art and had shown me basically how a computer works, I quickly realized that I needed to learn some of the basics of creating computer art before I could begin to find my way.

So, I returned to the computer, turned it on, and called out two words, "Vincent, help!"

The direct approach worked. In just a few seconds, Vincent appeared, looking as surrealistic as ever.

"I've been waiting for you to call me," he said with mock indignation. "I had begun to think you didn't need me any more."

ntals

ART

"I'm sorry," I said, trying my best to look remorseful. "I've been so busy cleaning up the warehouse and moving in that I haven't had a chance to start working on any computer art . And now that I *am* ready to start, I really need your help."

Vincent was easily appeased. "That's all right," he said, looking around the room. "Say, I hardly recognize the place. You *have* been busy."

"Do you like it?" I asked, eager for his approval.

"I do," Vincent looked down at the main room, with its clean, freshly painted walls and discrete, but effective, lighting. "You have some intriguing art on display."

"Most of that's mine," I said.

"And now you want to produce computer art, but you don't know where to begin."

I nodded. "I know we talked about a lot of techniques and theories a few weeks ago, but now I need some basic how-to instruction to get started."

"Of course," Vincent agreed. "Just as when you studied to become an artist, you started out by learning some basic concepts. So now I'll teach you some fundamentals of computer art."

"Thank you," I said with relief.

"Now then," Vincent said as the computer brought up a blackboard, "I'm going to cover three main areas that should give you the foundation you need in computer art." He began writing. "The first is raster graphics versus vector graphics."

"I remember touching on that a bit when you took me through the history of computer art," I said.

"Right. But today, we'll cover those in much greater depth," Vincent said. "We'll also look at 2-D versus 3-D, again adding to what I explained to you a few weeks ago. The other area we need to study is image quality." He turned from the blackboard. "That can have quite an effect on the output of your computer art."

I nodded.

"Working with a raster-based graphics is like painting on the screen, pixel by pixel."

"First, let's define raster graphics," Vincent began as the computer brought up a painting on an easel. "Raster-based imagery on the computer is best related to an oil painting. If you're working on an oil painting, the only way you can make a change is either by removing the paint itself or going over the top of it with new paint.

"Working with a raster-based graphics is like painting on the screen, pixel by pixel," Vincent continued as a graphic came up on the computer screen. "This is

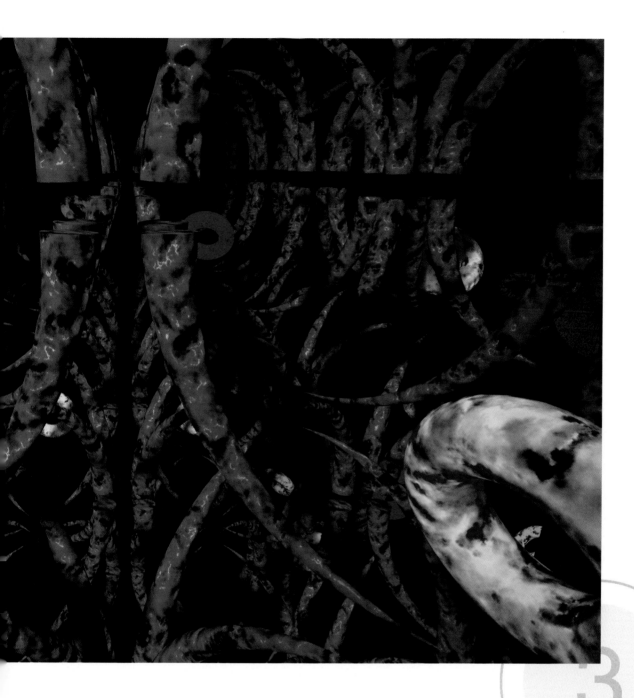

 is the decorative chapter number "3" at the right margin.

where the frame buffer comes in; we talked about frame buffers in the history lesson. This provides the memory you need to view the image while you're working on it. You can adjust the color, change the color values, or make other changes using different types of tools."

"Such as?"

"Well, most raster programs include paint-brushes, pencils, airbrushes, and so on — basically some of the same tools you have at your art table," Vincent replied as he pointed them out on the computer. "They also feature pixel enhancement tools, which can change the overall color value of the image, or just part of it."

"Besides enhancing images you create in vector programs, are there other applications for raster programs?" I asked.

"Sure," Vincent replied. "You might work with a painting you created using traditional methods or perhaps a photograph. You scan these images into digital form, then you can work with them in the computer's raster program."

"If raster programs are mostly for manipulating images, would vector programs be for the drawing itself?" I reasoned.

"You're always thinking ahead, aren't you?" Vincent smiled broadly. "Vector-based programs are object-oriented."

"What does that mean?"

"Well, say you're creating an image using these cut-outs of paper for a 3-D-type sculpture picture," Vincent said, holding up a sample. "You can rip, tear, squeeze, stretch, wad up, or move them around. Vector-based graphics work the same way; you're using and working with objects."

"I get it now," I said.

"As with all programs, there are some pros and cons to vector-based graphics," Vincent continued. "With an object-oriented graphic, it's broken down into a line of code that says 'Draw a line from XY coordinate here to XY coordinate there, and make it 1 pt. thick.' The one line of code that describes the line is extremely small; it doesn't take up a lot of memory."

"On the other hand, say you have a raster image with a resolution that is 600 pixels by 480 pixels." Vincent said. "That image has to be saved in the pixel format, one pixel at a time."

"Which would take up a lot of memory, right?" I asked.

"Right," Vincent replied. "There is a line of code for each pixel that is in the graphic. The more lines of code, the more memory that image requires. This is why a scanned image is going to take up a lot of memory; it is a raster graphic. A file from a vector program won't be that large because it's just a few lines of code, relatively speaking anyway. Those lines of code describe the shape and position of the objects — the polygons, squares, circles — that make up the image."

"Would you say, then, that it's better to work with vector graphics than raster?" I asked.

"Not necessarily," Vincent replied. "Instead, what's important is that you understand what you want to accomplish and what type of program will best help you reach that goal. In many cases, you can create a vector-based graphic, render it into a raster image, then use the raster tools to further enhance the image."

"What's important is that you understand what you want to accomplish and what type of program will best help you reach that goal."

"So you get the best qualities of both," I reasoned.

Vincent nodded. "Let's go back to the 3-D paper cut-outs analogy. There's only so much you can do with those objects. But in a raster program, you have tools like a paintbrush or airbrush. The freedom of using the brush stroke or the airbrush creates the random or organic-type look that can't be easily achieved when using object-based graphics."

"Can you give me an example combining raster and vector techniques?" I asked.

"Sure," Vincent replied. "Say you want to create an airbrush painting. First, you have to cut out a mask; let's say that mask is cut out in the shape of a square. Then, you fill it with a certain amount of color and gradation. Many programs will allow you to fill an object with just a solid color or a gradation of color. Some programs allow you to put images inside those objects. Those images could be graphics that you scanned in and maybe have created from a conventional airbrush."

"So you have a square in a vector program, but it's filled with a raster type image." I said.

"Yes, Vincent replied. "The best graphics programs allow you to use some of both abilities — where you can work in a vector-type form, but also have the benefits of using raster imagery inside the program. Or vice versa."

"It seems to me that one of the most basic lessons you can learn is how best to make the computer work for you," I said. "You have to know which tools to use and when."

"Exactly!" Vincent exclaimed. "You catch on quick. Take 3-D imagery for example. If you want to have a high-end, 3-D-

looking piece, it doesn't always have to be done using three-dimensional tools."

"It doesn't?"

"No," Vincent replied. "Three-dimensional tools can enhance your image. Say you have a ball. In some 3-D programs, you can give the ball attributes and add lighting effects to make it look like chrome. Then the computer will render the final image for you. A lot of times, though, you don't have the time or shouldn't take the time to go through and model a 3-D object just to get one single image."

"What do you mean by model?" I asked.

"Well, I'll explain it through the analogy of an airbrush artist," Vincent said. "Let's say he's doing a photorealistic image of a very complex item. He's not going to go out and build a model of his subject matter and take a photo of it."

"That wouldn't make a lot of sense," I observed.

"Right," Vincent agreed. "So instead, the artist will use references that already exist. Or he takes photographs of things that exist and uses his eyes, creativity, and ability as an artist to produce images. You can create very realistic images

using the two-dimensional tools that are available on computers today."

"So does that mean you can create images in 2-D that look like they're in 3-D?"

"Sure," Vincent replied, holding up a stunningly realistic image. "A lot of artists don't see how you can create images like this using traditional 2-D tools. It's simply a matter of sitting back and really analyzing what it is you're trying to create and figuring out the best way to create it.

"Take this picture, for instance," Vincent continued. "There's

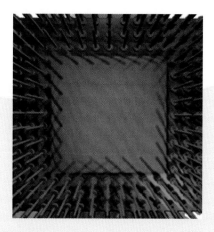

ILLUSTRATION

RESOLU

INDEPEN

OBJECTS

presentation

object oriented

true color

soft shadows

design

simply no way I'm going to model a car in a 3-D program to get a single image. That's like telling me to build a car with my hands. Creating the image using 2-D tools is the only feasible way to do it in a given time-frame."

"That sounds reasonable," I acknowledged.

"Now then, let's talk about interpolation," Vincent continued. "This will be a more practical discussion than the one we had a few weeks ago."

I nodded.

"Say I draw a square on the computer. Then I draw a rectangle," Vincent said. "Interpolation is telling the computer to determine a value that lies between the two known values of the square and the rectangle through a mathematical calculation. This process creates a repetition of new objects in between the two original one. That's one form of interpolation; there are lots of others."

"Such as?"

"Well, in some programs, you can't fill a vector-based object with a raster graphic or a gradient," Vincent replied. "In that case, you would need to use interpolation to create the gradient. As a matter of fact, interpolation was the only way you could create certain kinds of effects years ago in a vector-based program.

"Let's go back to my example," he continued. "That square is filled with red, and the rectangle next to it is filled with white. If I interpolate between them, it's also going to interpolate the color differences between the two and create what appears to the eye as a gradient."

"That's pretty slick," I noted.

"You bet it is," Vincent said. "That's part of the beauty of vector graphics. You're working with objects. What many artists don't realize a lot of times is that vector-based programs have the capabilities to render objects."

"The process of building is what's called modeling in 3-D art."

"You've mentioned rendering a couple of times," I said. "What exactly is it?"

"Rendering is the process of converting a vector-based graphic into a raster-based graphic," Vincent replied. "It's simple by definition, but the process is not. It requires some pretty complex mathematical calculations."

"But why would you want to render a vector graphic into a raster image?" I asked. "Aren't vector graphics easier to work with in some ways?"

"Yes," Vincent replied. "But as I've said before, there's only so much you can do with an object-oriented graphic. On the other hand, there are all sorts of possibilities when you bring those objects into a raster-based program.

"What this means is you get the best of both worlds," he continued. "In a vector-based program, you don't have an airbrush tool. You can't add highlights, blur, or make little adjustments to the image. But you can do all those things in a raster program."

"I think I understand now," I said. "Raster and vector each have unique capabilities, and there is a purpose for which one you choose."

"Right," Vincent said. "I want you to understand, though, that if you're going to use a vector program, do as much as you can with the graphic in vector first — only because it gives you so much more freedom to work with the design of your piece. Picking an object and moving it around and doing whatever you want to it is not as easy in raster because the

3

60

process doesn't allow as much freedom. Raster programs limit the level of changes you can make, if any. Take the image as far as you can in the vector program; render the image into a raster program and do whatever else you want with it."

"I think I understand the relationship between raster and vector now," I said. "Is it a similar one with 2-D and 3-D?"

"In a sense, yes," Vincent replied. "As with all the tools available to the computer artist, you need to understand which one is best suited for what you're trying to accomplish. It's the same whether you're comparing raster or vector, 2-D or 3-D."

"We've already talked about two-dimensional tools, haven't we?" I asked.

"Sure. Creating two-dimensional art on the computer isn't that much different from creating it using traditional methods," Vincent said. "But 3-D is an entirely different ball game."

"Why is that?"

"Because in 3-D, you have to build a model of the image you're trying to create," Vincent replied. "Consider, for example, the classic artist's still life — a bowl of fruit and a chair. I can paint the bowl of fruit and the chair. Or I can build them, and then take a photograph of what I've built.

"If I paint the fruit and chair, I'm using two-dimensional tools; if I build them, I'm using three-dimensional tools. Then, when I take the picture, I render it, to use the analogy."

"It sounds similar to the raster-versus-vector approach," I remarked.

"Right; it's a complete parallel," Vincent agreed. "The process of building is what's called modeling in 3-D art. You basically have a number of objects that you assemble — just like in a vector graphics program — and when you take a photograph, you've rendered it."

"Bit depth refers to the level of information, or the number of bits used to define each pixel on the screen."

"I can understand how you could build a model in the real world," I said. "but what about on a computer?"

"Well generally, you start with a two-dimensional cross-section," Vincent explained. "For example, if you were going to build the chair from the still life analogy, you could draw a square to represent one of its legs."

I was a bit skeptical, "A square?"

"Sure; if you're looking down at the top of the leg, that's all it is — a square," Vincent replied.

I nodded, conceding the point.

"Okay then, once I've built the square, I can take that into the three-

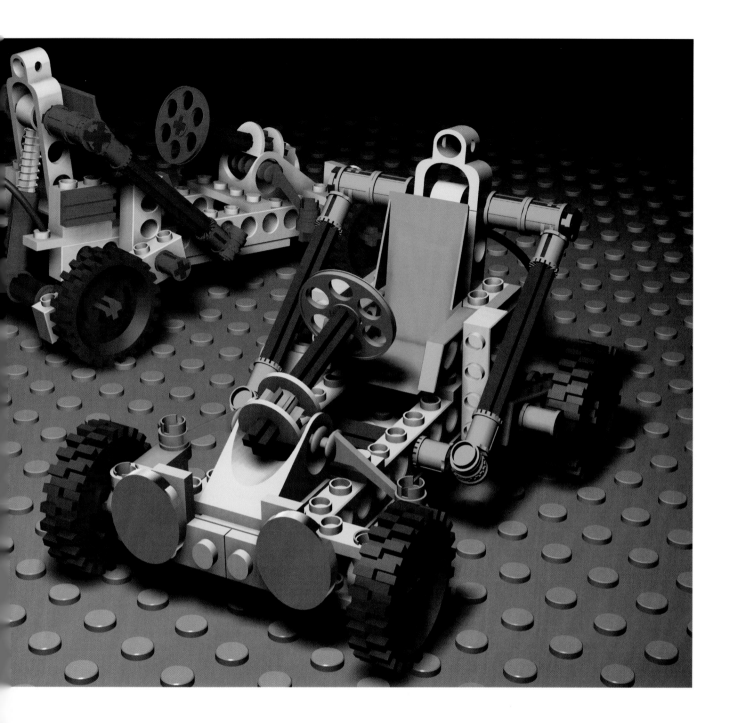

dimensional characteristics of the program and extrude it along the z-axis. All you're doing, basically, is stretching it out. As I stretch out the square, it builds a plane on the x-, y-, and z-axes for each face. Now, you've got a three-dimensional rectangle or a box that has been extruded along the z-axis."

"That's pretty ingenious — and simple at the same time," I remarked.

"Aha! You've hit on the key word," Vincent exclaimed. "Simple. No

matter what you're creating, no matter what the final shape may be, you have to break it down into it's simplest form to get it to a 3-D form.

"You can apply the process I've just explained to just about any polygon," Vincent continued. "A sphere, however, is a different process."

"How so?"

"Well, you start with either a circle or a half circle," Vincent replied.

"That's the two-dimensional shape you begin with. Then, you rotate it around the y-axis, connecting the faces as you go along to create the sphere. This is known as the surface of revolution."

"Is this the only way to model objects?" I asked.

"No, there are many other methods" Vincent replied. "But I'd rather not go into 3-D at length right now. It's an entirely different process, and you need to understand 2-D first. The important thing to know in working with 3-D is that you have to create models."

"But in some cases, it doesn't make sense because you can achieve the same effect in far less time using 2-D tools, right?" I asked.

"Definitely; you have to really think about what tools are going to be most appropriate," Vincent said. "It's like that painting I showed you earlier. You wouldn't try to build a model of the car from scratch. But you can paint it in 2-D and end up with a very nice image."

"That makes sense."

"The same principle applies to modeling," Vincent continued. "If you only want a single image for illustration purposes, why model it unless it's going to be easier to do it that way?"

"So when should you want to model your image?"

"It takes some thought. You need to be sure it's not easier to achieve what you want using two-dimensional tools," Vincent said. "But if you need to see the object from many different views and many different angles, or you want to animate it, then it probably will be much better to model it. If not, two-dimensional tools could do the trick."

"I think I understand how to build models and when you should," I said. "But once you've built the model, can you do anything with it in the 3-D program?"

"I was just about to get to that," Vincent replied. "After you've built your model, you can then tell the computer what you want to do with the surfaces of that model. You can give it a color. You

"A pixel is the basic quantum unit of an image when you break it into a grid, as in a raster program."

can create shading, two types of which are Gouraud or Phong."

"Named after the people who developed the process, right?"

"You remember well from the history lesson," Vincent smiled. "You can also bump map the surface, or texture map it with a raster-based image. There are a lot of things you can do with that surface. You can even ray trace it. However, once you render this vector-based graphic — which is the wireframe — it is converted to a raster format. Going back to the bowl of fruit and chair, it's the process of taking a photograph of what you've built."

"The enhancements you make to the model — is that what image quality is about?" I asked.

"No, image quality is sort of a separate issue," Vincent replied.

"Sort of?"

Vincent hedged. "Well, on the one hand, the issues involved with image quality are distinct from raster, vector, 2-D, or 3-D. At the same time, image quality issues have to be considered regardless of the type of graphic you're producing."

"What are some of the issues?" I persisted.

"One of the more common issues is bit depth," Vincent replied. "Bit depth refers to the level of information, or the number of bits used to define each pixel on the screen. The more information, the more possibilities for color.

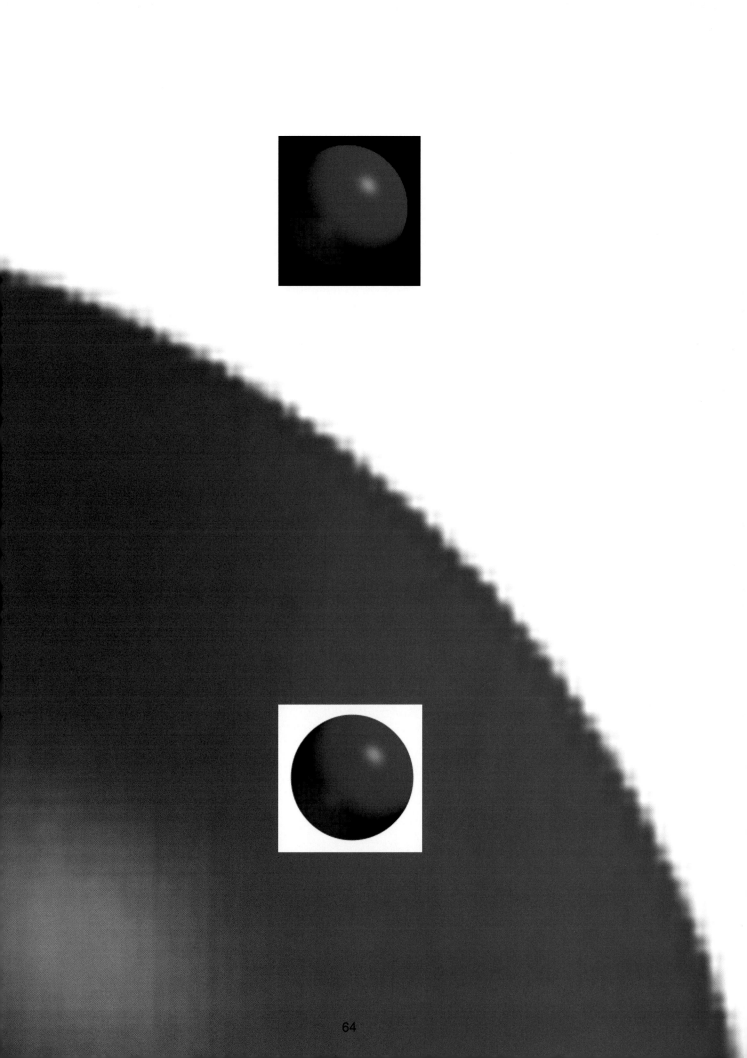

"I'll give you an analogy,"

Vincent said. "Do you know

anything about photography?"

"Originally, there was only black and white. Then it grew to four colors, and later to 16," he continued. "With 8-bit color, you could choose from 256 colors; 16-bit gave you thousands of colors; and with 24-bit, there were millions of colors from which to choose."

"I understand the choice of colors now available," I said. "But I don't understand how you get them."

"Okay. Well, first I should define a pixel," Vincent replied. "A pixel is the basic quantum unit of an image when you break it into a grid, as in a raster program. Pixels are very discrete, square, modular units, and they're usually organized in a rectangular matrix. It's like a sheet of graph paper. The entire matrix of these pixels is called a bitmap."

"Which is distinct from bit depth, right?"

"Yes. In reference to bit depth, when you have a pixel, it exists in planes; to expand the analogy, the more planes you have, the more chances for more colors," Vincent explained. "It's an additive process; the more layers you have, the more complex color you can achieve."

"Is this the highest level?" I asked. "Not that millions of colors doesn't give you enough choices."

"There is another step up, which is 32-bit," Vincent explained. "The 8 extra bits over 24-bit color create what's known as the alpha channel. The alpha channel is useful in compositing your image. It gives the computer additional memory and processing power to work with images in higher color modes.

"Another issue with pixels is spatial resolution. This represents the number of pixels used to create an image from top to bottom." Vincent continued. "If it's 30x40, 1000x1000, 1000x2000, or whatever, that's the resolution of your image."

"I've heard of high-resolution images," I said. "What's the threshold for that?"

"Well, it's open for debate," Vincent replied. "Normal video resolution is 512x486, and anything above that is generally considered high resolution. But now you can achieve resolutions that are much higher, and they continue to grow. So it's hard to pin down the standard. This brings up another issue, aspect ratio."

"Isn't that a geometric term?" I asked.

Vincent nodded. "Basically, it's your horizontal resolution compared to your vertical resolution. That's all an aspect

Vincent nodded. "Anti-aliasing is taking those pixels around that diagonal, and doing an averaging process between it and the background."

"Isn't that similar to interpolation?"

"You could say that. For example, if the diagonal line is supposed to be black, when you anti-alias it, the pixel next to it is going to be somewhat transparent and/or gray if the background is white," Vincent explained as the image was anti-aliased. "What this does is give the appearance of a straight diagonal line if your resolution is high enough."

"So that solves the problem of jaggies," I said, pointing to the now straight line in the hologram.

"Yes, but you should know that while it gets rid of one problem, it creates another," Vincent cautioned. "Some images or lines can become fuzzy or look fuzzy when they're anti-aliased."

ratio is, really, a comparison of horizontal to vertical, and it's the same in computer graphics," he said. "Another major issue regarding image quality is aliasing and anti-aliasing."

I looked at him with mild bewilderment. "You sure have some strange terms," I said. "I can't even begin to figure out what those mean."

"I'll try to explain it with an illustration," Vincent said as the computer brought up an image of a diagonal line. "Imagine drawing a diagonal line out of squares," he said as the image zoomed in to show how the line had been created. "Depending on your resolu-tion, the more stair-stepped your image is going to look. This effect," he said, pointing to the line, "is aliasing, also known as jaggies. The lower the resolution of your image, the more jaggy it's going to look."

"Let me venture a guess," I said. "Anti-aliasing is a way to eliminate the jaggies."

"And the resulting image?"

"It would be complete, crisp, and clear when it composites," Vincent replied.

"What if you don't have the alpha channel?" I asked.

"Where do those extra 8 bits you get with the alpha channel come in?" I asked.

"The alpha channel carries information with the pixel, which allows you to adjust the degrees of transparency for compositing the pixels over the top of something else," Vincent replied.

"You've lost me," I said.

"In layman's terms, for programs that address the alpha channel, you have more control over your image," Vincent explained. "The alpha channel can control the anti-aliasing around the edges of the object. It adjusts the anti-aliasing so that it blends into the background color.

"You can also create additional effects adjusting degrees of transparency for compositing over the top of other images," he continued. "For example, if you have a blue sphere with a complete black background and you have alpha channel information, you would be able to composite that image over the top of another one with no problems."

"If you're compositing that image over the top of another one, what you might be able to do in the program is only make the black clear," Vincent explained. "While you made the black transparent, you were actually able to put that sphere over the top and composite it with the other image.

"Now go back to anti-aliasing issues," he continued. "If you're compositing this blue sphere with a black background, that sphere has those averaged pixels around it."

"And won't those show up since they're a different color?"

"Sure they will. Because when you anti-aliased it originally, you did it to black. You didn't anti-alias it to the new background that you're putting it on," Vincent explained. "So when you composite one image over the top of another, and you don't have the alpha channel, the anti-aliasing shows up and it makes the image look terrible."

"So in other words, for high-quality edges in compositing, the additional information that's handled by the alpha channel makes it better," I remarked.

"Right," Vincent said. "That brings us to another issue that affects the quality of your image when you have it output: the rendering process."

"That's when you convert vector information into raster, right?"

Vincent nodded. " When you render an image, a lot of times you can adjust the resolution of the raster image," he said. "For example, you can render an image out as a 2000x2000-pixel or -line file. This is your first generation image taken from vector into raster." The computer brought up a sample image.

"Now, that 2000x2000-line file may not have a high enough resolution for the output you want," Vincent continued. "In some programs, you can *res* the file up to a higher resolution."

"Which means?"

"You render that image up to a 4000x4000-line file," Vincent said. "What you're doing is spreading your image out over a larger area. It really doesn't do that much good. Just because it's bigger doesn't necessarily mean it's better."

"So then, what do you do?" I asked.

"I'll give you an analogy," Vincent said. "Do you know anything about photography?"

"A little," I replied.

"The film size most commonly used is 35 millimeter," Vincent said. "It does a good job for a variety of photographic applications, just like a 2000x2000-line image. But if you're taking a photo of something that you plan to blow up extra large..."

"A 35-millimeter image will become grainy," I interrupted.

Vincent nodded. "So for big prints, a photographer will shoot with a larger 4x5 inch film to achieve the quality he's after," he said. "By the same token, if you know you want your final image to have a 4000x4000-line resolution, you should go back to your vector file and render it out at that resolution."

"That way, you get the quality you want from the beginning," I said.

"Exactly."

Vincent paused for a minute. "I think we've done enough talking about these ideas," he said. "Why don't we try creating a few images?"

I rolled my chair over to the computer screen. "I thought you'd never ask."

creating

compu

For the next several weeks, it seemed that I spent almost every waking minute either in my studio at the computer or at the computer store. Taking Vincent's advice, I sampled a variety of both raster and vector programs.

With each new software purchase, Vincent and I would spend several hours experimenting with the programs, creating some simple, basic images. One of

the first things we discovered was that while the programs had several features and capabilities in common, there was also some unique terminology for each.

"All these different terms are getting me confused," I finally admitted. "It's reaching the point where I'm not sure which tool to use for what effect. Do you think you could give me a quick rundown of the main tools and what they're used for."

"Sure," Vincent replied. "It's easy to become overwhelmed by all the choices you have. Remember the experiences of early computer artists such as Lillian Schwartz? But of course, she didn't have me around."

"We'll start by looking at raster, which is sometimes referred to as paint pro-

mages

on the

ter

4

grams," Vincent began. "The cropping or cut tool is used to delete unwanted background information. Or you can use it to save sections of the image as separate files or to composite."

"What exactly is compositing?" I asked.

"Using the compose or composite tool, you can take an existing image and place it over the top of another," Vincent replied. "This tool has the capability of creating certain effects."

"Such as?"

"You might change certain colors, or the lightness values of the pixels in the image you are compositing. It can be extremely effective."

"What's this icon that looks like a little lasso?" I asked.

"That tool goes by several names, one of which is lasso," Vincent replied. "It's also known as the polygon tool, and it allows you to segment a certain part of the image for enhancement or manipulation. The rectangle or circle tool has the same function."

"Moving right along, we come to the fill tools," Vincent continued. "These are used to fill areas selected by the various shape tools I just described. The fill tool, sometimes called the seed fill or smart fill, can also fill areas according to a pixel's hue, saturation, and lightness values."

"Which would allow you to modify the color," I said.

"I'll give you an example," Vincent said. "Say the pixels in your image consist of mostly gray with a little black. You could use the fill tool to change the various shades of gray without affecting the black, or to vary dark values. The fill might consist of a gradient, solid, or transparent color."

"In some of my experimentation, particularly with scanned images, I've come across blemishes or parts of the image I don't want to include," I said. "How do I get rid of those?"

"You could use the clone or rubber stamp tool to duplicate another section of the image to the desired spot," Vincent replied. "Another useful tool is the filter, or special effects tool, which you can use to create — surprise, surprise — special effects. You might want to blur, sharpen, or emboss your image, maybe create a mosaic or ripple effect, or even create what I call visual noise."

"And I can control just how much these effects alter my image?"

"Sure, special effects tools are always a matter of degree," Vincent replied. "So are your image control tools. These let you adjust the color, brightness, contrast, and saturation—all concepts you already understand."

"There are just a couple other major tools in raster," Vincent continued. "Your airbrush, of course, lets you lay down a diffused spray of color on top of an image. You've used a conventional airbrush, haven't you?"

I nodded.

"And you can use the paint brush tool to paint a soft or hard edge," Vincent said. "The last major tool in raster is a mask."

"I've used those with a conventional airbrush," I said. "It's just a way to isolate part of an image and apply color changes, filters, or other effects."

"And it basically works the same way on the computer," Vincent said. "Now, in your vector programs, you have some different tools and terminology. Because vector involves building objects, which are often layered over each other, you have to rank your objects in priority. You can either send objects to the front or to the back. Usually, your smaller objects go in front of the larger ones."

Vision: The completed image.

"For building those objects, you might use the polygon, spline, rectangle, square, ellipse, or circle tool," Vincent continued. "This lets you create a closed shape with either straight or curved sides. Then you can fill the shape with a solid color, a gradient, and in some programs, an image."

"Perhaps something you've scanned in?" I asked.

Vincent nodded. "Now say you've already built an object.

"Special effects tools

are always

a matter of degree."

Your edit points or spline let you alter that shape."

"Are interpolation and blend the same thing?" I asked.

"Yes, it's just a term that varies from program to program. Some programs call it space," Vincent replied. "In a two-dimensional program, interpolation lets you select two different shapes, and the computer will create a specified number of shapes between the two selected forms. It will adjust or morph between the two."

"And you can interpolate across multiple properties of the object?"

"Sure; your changes can range from shape, color, size, placement, or transparency depending on the program," Vincent replied. "Interpolation lets you introduce or insert additional values between the existing values in a series."

"There are other major tools in a vector program that are self-explanatory," Vincent continued. "Things like scale, rotation, and duplication. The attributes menu lets you select what you might use to fill or outline an object."

"And all vector programs have these tools?" I asked.

Vision, Process 1: White text on black background; adding an automatic gradient.

"Those are the basics. Some programs might have some additional alteration tools, but these vary from program to program," Vincent explained. "Tools that allow you to mirror or flop an image on the x- or y-axis. Some programs have a slant tool, which allows you to create slants or a skew on the x- or y-axis, too."

"What about the z-axis?"

"That's in the realm of 3-D," Vincent replied. "As I've said before, creating 3-D is an entirely different process."

"So we're not going to create any images in 3-D?" I had been looking forward to that.

"Not really, not for now," Vincent replied. "You really need to master creating 2-D images first. However," he continued, sensing my dis-

appointment, "because you've been learning so well, I guess I could define some of the terms related to 3-D, and maybe show you some of the basics involved in creating a simple 3-D object."

"Thanks, Vincent."

"Now then, in 3-D, a point extended in one direction becomes a line, and a line extended along a second axis forms a plane," he began. "This is a two-dimensional surface. If you extend a plane along a perpendicular axis, it forms a volume."

"This is part of the modeling process, right?"

"You might say that," Vincent replied. "Modeling is actually a mathematical description of a three-dimensional object. Remember how early computer graphics were all algorithms? Modeling uses mathematical

equations to define shape, dimensions, color, surface, and texture."

"Can you walk me through the modeling process?" I asked. "Just the basics."

"One way of creating a model is to start with a section or a cross section of a volume," Vincent explained. "You do this by creating a polygon in most cases."

"Is this the same as creating polygons in 2-D?"

Vincent nodded. "Once you have your 2-D polygon, you can choose from multiple methods to create a volume or the 3-D shape," he continued. "Extrusion is the process of taking a two-dimensional object and extending it along a third axis. This creates a solid shape. Your circle becomes a cylinder. A square becomes a box."

I nodded in understanding.

"Another method for creating 3-D is surface of revolution," Vincent said. "The revolution of a plane on any given axis creates a solid shape."

"Are their ways to apply 3-D effects to a 2-D image?" I asked.

"There are a couple of mapping techniques that will accomplish

> "In 3-D, a point extended in one direction becomes a line, and a line extended along a second axis forms a plane."

"Bump mapping creates the illusion of physical surface characteristics or bumps on a 3-D surface."

that. You can take a 2-D image and map it onto a three-dimensional surface," Vincent explained. "Some of the most common mapping procedures are texture mapping for colors or textures and bump mapping."

"The technology developed by James Blinn, right?"

Vincent nodded. "Bump mapping creates the illusion of physical surface characteristics or bumps on a 3-D surface. Other mapping techniques include reflection or environment mapping, which reflect surrounding elements. And transparency mapping causes the model to become transparent where a certain pixel value in the map might be found, usually black. Actually, there's a lot more to this, but I think we should save an in-depth discussion of 3-D for later."

"That's fine," I replied. "At least you've given me something to think about for the future."

Although Vincent and I had experimented with the different programs for a few weeks now, we hadn't really concentrated on creating a complete image. Now that I felt more comfortable with the various tools available, I thought it was time to try, and Vincent agreed.

There was only one problem. What kind of image did I want to create?

"I've been running a lot of potential images through my head as you've been teaching me," I told Vincent, "but no idea has really reached out and grabbed me yet."

"That's to be expected. It can be tough coming up with an idea, whether or not you're using the computer."

"I know; this isn't the first time I've had this problem," I acknowledged. "But like you've said before, the computer presents so many tools and capabilities, your mind just goes wild. Not only do I have to work through the creative issues I'm used to dealing with, I have to adjust to an entirely new set of tools. It's just a different process for realizing my vision."

It was as if a light bulb had gone off in Vincent's head. "Well then, why don't we make that your first computer image?" he exclaimed.

"Make what my first image?" I asked. Even after spending so much time together, Vincent's train of thought still escaped me sometimes.

"Vision!" Vincent exclaimed. "We can take that simple word and create all sorts of effects with it."

While Vincent's enthusiasm could be quite contagious, I couldn't yet see the spark of an idea that had already caught fire in his mind. "You think so?" I asked.

Vincent was not to be denied. "All we're going to do is take the experimenting we've done a step further. We'll simply try some different effects and combine them. You can do it. Honest."

It was certainly better than no idea, which was all I had at that point. "Okay, let's give it a shot."

Opening one of the vector programs, I typed the word "vision" using the text tool.

"Since we're going to create several effects on this type, should I make it white over a black background?" I asked.

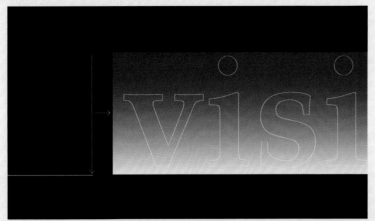

Vision, Process 2: Interpolating the gradient using purple and yellow.

Vincent nodded. "Let's start by creating a gradient."

"That's easy," I said. "This program can create a color gradient inside the text automatically. I think I'll go from purple to yellow."

"But not every program has that capability," Vincent pointed out. "Pop quiz — how could else you create a gradient?"

"Interpolation." Unlike some of my art classes, I had paid attention during Vincent's lessons.

"Good answer. Unfortunately, it's a lot more difficult," Vincent said. "You have to interpolate the gradient and create masks of black around it to make it appear as if the letters are there."

"Let's try it anyway," I said. "Say I indicate a purple line at the top and a yellow line at the bottom. I can interpolate between the two of those to create a gradient that's behind the type. Then my outline of the text goes in front."

"So far, so good," Vincent said. "Now comes the tricky part. Take your polygon tool and build a black mask using the text image for reference."

Vincent was right. It was tricky. And time consuming.

"Now I see why you wouldn't want to do it

"Let's start by creating a gradient."

this way," I said after I had finally traced out part of the "v" in "vision."

"Well, there's another reason," Vincent said. "It also creates a layering problem, because the word "vision" doesn't exist as an object anymore."

"It doesn't?"

"No, it's a series of masks," Vincent replied. "As a result, you can't layer things underneath it or use the edge of the text as an edge to go behind. And if you rank anything behind it, it's going to go behind the black mask also."

"What other option do you have?" I asked. "If you have to create your gradient using interpolation, there ought to be some way to work around this masking problem."

"Well, in some vector programs there is a third option," Vincent said. "It's a tool that lets you create a mask out of the text itself. What this means is you go through and create the gradient you had done by interpolating two objects. The difference is, the program will let you select the text and make it into a mask itself."

"It sounds like the same process I just went through," I remarked.

"It is. Only now it's automatic."

"All the same, I think I'll stick with just selecting the text and letting the program create the gradient inside the text." And with that, I closed the file on my partially completed interpolated gradient.

Vincent and I returned to the first gradient I had

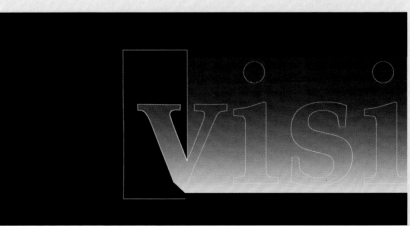

Vision, Process 3: Adding a black mask to trace the text.

Vision, Process 5: Beveling text edges.

created on the word "vision."

"Let's duplicate that text on top of itself," Vincent suggested. "Then, go into the image attributes menu and change the image that's in the back."

"What should we change it to?"

tion with the program. "If I go into the attributes menu of the text, I can indicate that I want a gradient inside. But I can also indicate that I want the text to

some dimension. It doesn't pop yet."

"Well, what would you suggest?" Vincent leaned back. "This is your image, and I want you to continue applying what you've learned. Take the initiative."

Vincent was right. I peered critically at the image for a minute or two. "Maybe we could bevel the letters. Create a little bit of shininess," I suggested finally.

"That sounds good," Vincent said. "Why don't you start by drawing some polygonal shapes around the blue/green edges of letters and fill them with the other gradients."

Vision, Process 4: Layering the text images to create an edge around the whole text.

"Turn off the gradient on the interior," Vincent replied. "Then, let's change its line width to a different color — blue/green perhaps — and increase it. Now, you've got an edge around the whole text."

"I think there's another way to create this effect," I said, remembering some of my earlier experimenta-

have a specific line width."

"It's good to see you applying the things I've taught you," Vincent noted.

I looked at the image we had created for a minute of two. "I like what we've got so far," I said. "But I think we need to create

"We could go between the blue/green color of the outline, a lighter version of the blue/green, and then back to the original color," I said as I worked. "And since this program can fill objects with a color gradient, I'm not going to go through the hassle of interpolation."

"Good choice. I don't feel like being here all day."

Vision, Process 6: Adding highlighting gradients and refining the beveled edges.

As I went through the process of creating the gradients around the letters, I noticed that in some areas, the edges I had created made it look like a bevel. But in other places, I had created edges where I didn't really want them.

"What do I do with these edges that I don't want?" I asked, annoyed at this unexpected snag.

"Leave it for now," Vincent replied. "Remember what I said earlier. You want to do as much as you can in the vector program. We can take care of those unwanted edges when we take the image over into a raster program."

Being something of a perfectionist, I hated to leave something that I saw as such an obvious flaw. But knowing Vincent was right, I resumed the process across the rest of the text. And as I worked, I could see the overall lighting effect. It also achieved the dimension I was after.

"Well, what do you think?" I asked after I finished.

Vincent nodded approvingly. "Now it's time to move on to another part of the image," he said. "Because we've created the gradients inside the text, that's easy to do."

"I'm curious, though. What if we had used the mask technique?" I asked, interested in knowing all the angles.

Vincent looked amused. "If you create this image using masks, you're going to have to save your image up to now as a separate file," he replied. "You can duplicate the text object from that file for reference only, making it solid white — or whatever color you want."

"Then, you'd go on and create the rest of the image in a new file," Vincent continued. "You'd have to composite your first

Vision, Process 7: Interpolating a background.

image with the second later in a raster-based program."

"But since we've created our image without masks, we don't have to worry about that," Vincent continued crisply. "What we want to do now is create a background behind the text."

"Won't that affect my text object?" I didn't want to accidentally mess it up.

"Not if you lock it down or hide it," Vincent replied. "Then you can work on other things without accidentally selecting those objects."

"I forgot that."

"You don't need to reference the text, so why don't you hide it for now?" Vincent suggested. "Any ideas for the background?"

I thought for a moment. "What if we interpolated between a couple of ellipses?" I suggested. "It could be black at the very outer edge, and maybe a dark blue at the center."

Vincent nodded approvingly as I created the interpolation. "I like it," he said. "Now, rank it behind your text object."

Once the background was complete, I un-hid the "vision" text and placed it on top of the background. "I still think it needs some added dimension," I noted. "What if I duplicated the text, made it black, and offset it in the background to create a shadow?"

Vision, Process 8: Duplicated black text for shadow effect.

"Try it, and see how it looks," Vincent replied. "You may also want to shrink it down just a little, too."

"That's the effect I was looking for," I said. "Now, it pops."

By now I was happy with the image Vincent and I had created.

Vision, Process 9: Adding the look of water droplets.

Still, I wanted to add something more. And besides, I hadn't even taken it into the raster program yet.

"What if you created an effect to look as if somebody had thrown water over the word vision?" Vincent suggested.

Now that was an interesting concept. "I can see it in my head," I said skeptically, "but I have no idea how I could do that on the computer."

Vincent just smiled calmly. "You can do it. It isn't even that hard."

"All right then, how do I start?" I was such a pushover.

"Let's begin by creating an abstract shape over to the left of the text," Vincent suggested. "Make it kind of bulbous, free-form, no straight edges. The object here is to be loose and to create something without really thinking about it too much."

"Now make the outside shape black in form," Vincent continued. "Let's shrink it down a little bit and edit our points on the inside shape."

"And then I could do some interpolation to

get a gradient between the two, right?" I asked.

"Yes," Vincent replied. "Why don't you make the color a variation on that blue/green, maybe with more green to it than what our background has."

"See?" Vincent exclaimed in triumph. "You drew your first water drop on the computer and it wasn't hard at all."

"You're right," I admitted. "I think I'll make some more."

Vincent nodded. "Just keep the shapes abstract and bulbous," he said. "You should probably make the shapes a bit smaller at the center and larger towards the edges of the image."

"Why?"

"Well, say you did splash some water on these letters," Vincent replied. "The water would probably break up more around the text, leaving larger puddles towards the outside."

"Okay," I said, building a series of loose shapes.

Some of the shapes I created were very round, others more abstract. I created a couple with holes, some without. I filled a few of the shapes as solid black; for others, I created linear gradients. I also interpolated between a couple of shapes so my gradients would have a center point.

Having created a series of water

droplets around the text, I got another idea.

"You know, if somebody splashed water on these letters," I said to Vincent, "there would probably also be some small water drops on the letters themselves."

"Good point," Vincent acknowledged. "But since these water droplets are against a brighter background, you should probably make the shapes transparent."

"I agree. But to make at least the outlines of the water drops visible, I can use a little bit of the blue green color from the text outlines, together with off white."

"You might also want to add a

little shadow edge to it in a darker shade of the blue/green," Vincent suggested. "Then add a small white polygon — anywhere in the water drop — so it looks like it's reflecting the light."

It took a little while to add all the water drops to the letters. But I was pleased with the result.

"I think we're basically through with what we can do to this image in the vector program," Vincent said. "Now let's take it to raster."

"Do I need to render this image?" I asked.

"Yes," Vincent replied. "But sometimes, the rendering process is just saving the file in a raster format. You'll need to make sure your raster program can read it. Then, when you open up the file in your raster program, it will automatically convert or render the image."

I saved the image, quit the vector program, opened the raster program and, just as Vincent had said, opened the saved image file.

"With the raster program, we can enhance those bulbous water shapes so they'll really stand out," Vincent explained.

"When you suggested I add the little white polygons to the water drops, it was as if they were reflecting off a light source," I said. "Maybe we could add some highlights."

"That's just what I was going to suggest," Vincent said. "It seems to me that the brightest point in the picture is in the center underneath the text. You'll need to take this into account when creating

highlights on the water. All the bright points on the water drops should be facing towards that light source."

"In my traditional artwork, I've used an airbrush to create highlights," I pointed out. "Wouldn't it be the same for the computer?"

Vincent nodded. "Have at it."

Selecting the airbrush tool, I sprayed a layer of white around the very curved edges of the water drops to create a highlight effect.

"May I make a suggestion?" Vincent asked as I continued to spray with the airbrush tool.

I didn't even look up from my work. "Sure."

"The highlights look great, especially in the center of the drops," Vincent began. "They'll really pop, though, if you make them very hard around the edges of the water. You can use your paintbrush tool to give it that hard edge on one side, leaving the other side soft."

Having completely airbrushed one of the water drops, I did as Vincent suggested, using black with my paintbrush. He was right. So I repeated the process for the remaining water drops.

Finally, I was done highlighting. I had been working so closely with the individual water drops that I was a bit surprised when I refreshed the screen to look at the complete image. Not that it was earth-shattering, but for my first attempt at creating an image on the computer, I certainly felt good about it.

Even if I did get some help.

Vision, Process 11: Adding water droplets to the text.

A few days after completing Vision, one of my clients came by my studio with a problem. Her company was developing a new camera, and needed pictures of it for the introductory advertising. However, the existing prototype looked too rough for product photos. She needed a realistic image for the ad — after all, this was a camera. Could I, she asked, draw a photorealistic image of their camera — at a reasonable cost?

The project sounded like just kind of the challenge I needed. Not only would this be an opportunity to expand my abilities in computer art, but this was a paying client with a decent budget.

Still, I didn't want to over-promise and end up with an unhappy client. I told her I would research and evaluate the project, then give her my recommendation and a quote to do the job. She was agreeable, so as soon as she left, I went to the computer and called for Vincent.

"I think we've found our next major project," I said as Vincent's image appeared. "I need to illustrate a prototype of a camera, and it has to look realistic — like a photograph. Can I use the tools I have and apply the lessons you've taught to achieve what my client wants?"

Vincent mused just long enough to make me nervous. Then he smiled. "Sure you can" he said. "In fact, there are several reasons why you might want to draw something to look like a photo using 2-D tools. Taking a good photograph of something can be much more expensive than having an illustrator draw it."

"Well, in our case, we have to create a realistic image for something that doesn't exist yet."

"It's still feasible," Vincent assured me, "as long as you have good references."

After Vincent had given me an idea of the time required to produce the image, I explained to my client what I was going to do, how much it would cost, and when I could have it completed. She approved the quote, and gave me the CAD dia-

"The more references you have the better. And it helps that these photos show the prototype from several angles."

photorealism. The more references you have the better. And it helps that these photos show the prototype from several angles."

"I have a camera looks a little bit like this one," I suggested. "That might help."

"Good idea," Vincent said. "It would give us a reference for the texture of the plastic."

I found a camera that looked similar to my client's, and using another camera, took several pictures from different angles. And at Vincent's suggestion, I photographed my other camera equipment, experimenting to see how the surfaces appeared at various angles and with different lighting. It took some time to develop the photos and organize all our references. But I had built this time into the quote at Vincent's suggestion, and it was necessary if I was to do the job right.

The Camera: The completed image.

grams of the new camera and some photos of the prototype for reference.

"These will work fine," Vincent said as he looked over my client's materials. "Having a good reference is the secret to creating

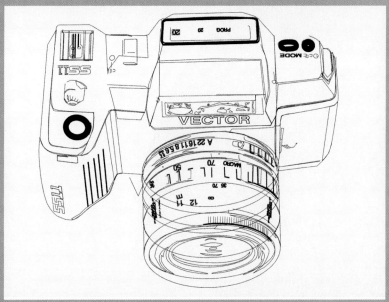

The Camera, Process 1: An outline drawn for reference.

"Well, we certainly have enough references," I said, examining the large pile. "Now, what's the best way to get these into the computer?"

"Why don't you start with that diagram," Vincent said, pointing to the top reference. "If you can project that image with a lucigraph — also known as a luci — or a slide projector, you can trace around the edges picking up shapes. You can also trace the highlights, dark spots, and light spots."

After having spent so much time at the computer lately, it felt strange to be working with a simple pencil and paper again. But as I traced, I noticed there were several details that differed between the prototype and the CAD diagrams.

"There really isn't anything representative for some parts of this camera," I pointed out.

"Why don't you talk to your client about the areas that aren't clear," Vincent suggested. "She might be able to describe some of those features."

After a couple of in-depth conversations with one of the camera's engineers, I had a better idea of what some of its less-defined features looked like. Once I had the outline complete, I scanned it into the computer.

"Some vector programs allow you to bring in a scanned image and lock it down in the background," Vincent said. "Then you can use it for reference for what you're going to draw on top of it. There is an alternative method, but it requires a digitizing tablet. And you don't have one."

"Well, what is it? Maybe I should get one." I didn't relish the prospect of tracing the outline all over again.

"A digitizing tablet is an input device you can use in place of a mouse," Vincent explained. "A mouse is a relative input device. In other words, there is no relationship between where it is on the table and where the cursor is on the screen."

"But there is a relationship with a tablet?"

"Yes. You can have a square tablet and when your cursor is on a certain position on the tablet, it's always on a corresponding position on the screen," Vincent continued.

"So if I had a digitizing tablet, I could simply tape down the picture onto on the tablet, and build my reference points into the computer directly," I said.

Vincent nodded. "Yes."

"I'd like to get one of those," I said. "I'll just have to see how it fits with my budget and the kind of work I'll be doing."

"Good idea," Vincent agreed. "It's tempting to buy a lot of equipment when you're doing computer graphics, but first, you

4

have to make sure you really need it and can justify the expense."

"Let's move on to building the image," Vincent continued. "There's a trick to building any type of image like this. It has to be free and open and loose. Some of your shapes won't really make sense."

"I'm not sure what you mean."

"When you look at your reference, look for light values and dark values," Vincent replied. "Just make a basic outline of what your shapes might be. As abstract as they might look now, you'll see the difference when we get to the final image."

"But if it's too abstract, I'll lose the accuracy I need," I protested.

"Oh, it will still be accurate," Vincent assured me. "You need an outline of the picture so you can draw it correctly and to put in those subtle variations of lights and darks that make a basic outline shape."

As I began to draw the camera on the computer, Vincent made another important suggestion.

"Draw the small pieces first," he explained. "It's best to start with the very small highlights or variations in shading and work backwards.

"In other words, don't draw the outline of the whole shape?" I asked.

"Right. Work with the small pieces first."

"Why?" I asked.

"Because vector programs work by building layers," Vincent explained. "Remember, you have your traced reference in the background of the screen. If you draw a great big outline of the image itself first, you'll cover up all your reference lines."

"So if I start with my small reference lines, I won't cover up anything before I need to reference it," I said, completing the thought. "That makes sense."

Following Vincent's instructions, I started drawing the smaller objects on the camera lens. At this point, things were basic. Besides drawing the shapes, I added some other lines, including the letters that would be on the actual lens. I created some grays, blacks, and highlights, picking various colors that might be close to the real thing. In a couple of places, I filled the objects with gradients.

"Should I lock these objects once I get them done?" I asked Vincent after I had finished with the lens. "It's taken me so long to draw the lens that I wouldn't want to accidentally alter anything."

"Yes; you can also group them as a single object," Vincent said. "And if you hide the

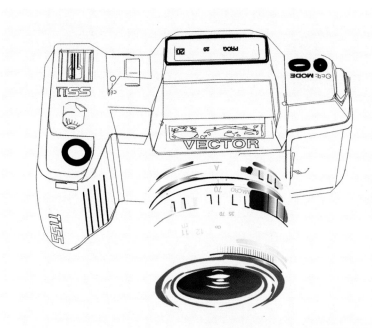

The Camera, Process 2: Working with small reference lines to define the lens.

**Following Vincent's instructions,
I started drawing
the smaller objects
on the camera lens.**

The Camera, Process 3: Using ellipses and gradients for the lens.

lens rather than just lock it, you can then still see all your reference points."

"Now it would be good to create a series of ellipses to represent the overall shape of the lens," Vincent explained. "Fill them with gradients or create the gradients using interpolation and

The Camera, Process 5: A nearly complete lens.

layer them one on top of the other from back to front."

"Wouldn't the end of the lens appear black?" I asked, pointing out one of the reference photos.

"Yes," Vincent replied. "Then you can group these objects together."

"I think we've got a problem," I remarked after I had layered the ellipses one on top of the other." There's a little gap between them. The outline of the lens is supposed to be uniform."

"No big deal," Vincent assured me. "All you have to do is draw a couple of small polygons where you see the gaps and fill them with the color of the ellipse behind them. That'll close them up."

"I'm curious to see what this looks like so far," I said after I had filled in the gaps and grouped the polygons together with the ellipses.

"Why don't I bring back my hidden objects?"

"I'm curious, too," Vincent said. "Go ahead."

With the two groups of images combined, I was happy to see we had the clear beginnings of the camera lens. Then, since I was working with layers and individual pieces, I grouped all the lens objects together and hid them away.

With the lens basically complete, I turned my attention to the front

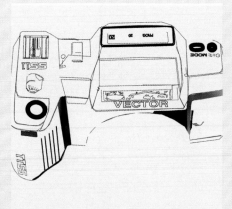

The Camera, Process 6: The lens hidden, adding detail to the front face.

face of the camera. Just as I had done with the lens, I built the smaller shapes first, working my way up to the larger objects.

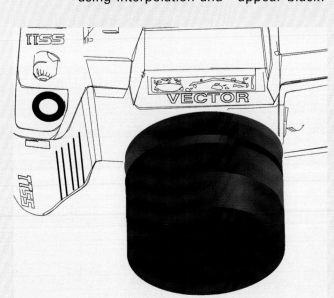

The Camera, Process 4: Smoothing the layered objects with small polygons.

"Now it would be good to create a series of ellipses to represent the overall shape of the lens."

The Camera, Process 7: Including a gradient to add further detail.

By now, I was becoming more adept. I remembered to layer the larger shapes behind the smaller ones without Vincent reminding me.

"Shouldn't the larger shapes include a gradient to simulate the effects of lighting on top of them?" I asked.

"You're really catching on," Vincent appeared pleased with my work. "Once you've created the gradients, you can layer those larger objects back behind the smaller shapes."

As I had done with the lens, I grouped and hid the objects that created the front face of the camera and began working on the top. Again, I built the small objects first.

The Camera, Process 10: Composite of smaller and larger objects.

One portion of the camera top gave me trouble, though — the lens for the flash attachment.

"It's such an abstract shape," I said. "I can't seem to nail it down here."

"Why don't you set it aside until we bring the image over into the raster program," Vincent suggested. "I think you'll be able to get a better handle on it then."

Having built all the smaller objects for the top of the camera, I repeated the process for the larger one. It was still a painstaking process, but it did seem that I was getting better at it.

Vincent had remained quiet as I finished the top of the camera. Even after I combined the small and large objects, he just observed with a slight smile. I took it as a good sign.

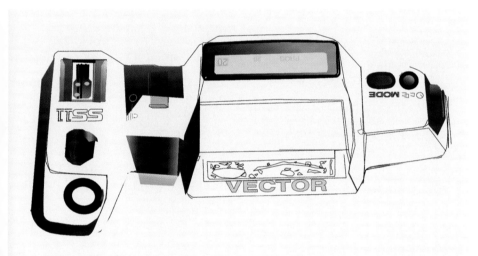

The Camera, Process 8: Defining and layering smaller objects.

One portion of the camera top gave me trouble, though — the lens for the flash attachment.

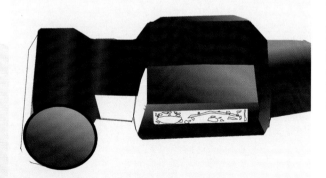

The Camera, Process 9: Building larger areas for the camera's top.

The Camera, Process 11: Un-hiding the lens.

Vincent broke his silence after I un-hid the lens and front of the camera to combine it with the top.

"That looks great," he said enthusiastically. "Now let's go over to the raster program and add those little touches that'll make it look even more realistic."

"Now that I've got the image in raster," I said as I opened my saved vector file in the raster program, "I should probably resolve the issue with the flash attachment lens."

"All right, we can do that. First, you'll need to create a mask so you don't paint in areas you don't want to," Vincent said.

I masked over all but the area where the flash attachment's lens would go. "What now?" I asked.

"Use your airbrush tool and spray down some abstract shapes within your unmasked area," Vincent replied. "That'll get you started."

Vincent then told me to add some more definable shapes using the paintbrush tool.

"Try to create what you might see on a flashbulb lens," he said.

I gave my own camera's flash attachment a hard look. Then, as best I could, I tried to transfer that mental image onto the image on my screen.

"There's just one more thing that will put the finishing touch on that lens," Vincent said. "Use your air-brush and spray a light tint of white in the upper-right corner over the top of the glass. That makes it look more realistic."

"I can think of something else I should do," I pointed out. "Just like on 'Vision,' I can see some edges that are too noticeable. The blur tool will smooth those edges out."

"I like this camera even better than the first image we did," I said when I finished.

"Of course you do," Vincent replied. "You're growing as an artist. This was a harder image, and you did more of it without my help."

"Even better, I'm getting paid for it."

The Camera, Process 12: Using a raster program to resolve finer details.

I can see some edges that are too noticeable. The blur tool will smooth those edges out.

The Camera, Process 13: Adding definition and realism using paintbrush and airbrush tools.

'57 Chevy: The completed image.

could paint a picture of his favorite, the 1957 Chevrolet.

"Even better," I suggested, "I'll do it on the computer."

Unlike the camera assignment, it would be easy to find a perfect reference for my image. Every Saturday evening, hundreds of classic car owners gathered at a local shopping center to show off their chrome-covered beauties. I found several '57 Chevys there, all of which I photographed from various angles.

Even though I had become increasingly confident creating

computer images, I still wanted Vincent's opinion and guidance. "What do you think would be the best perspective for drawing the car?" I asked.

Vincent surveyed the various references I had collected. "The back; definitely the back," he replied. "Those tail fins were the '57 Chevy's trademark."

"Good, that's what I was thinking, too."

My client was so happy with the completed camera image that I was eager to do another photorealisitc image. Fortunately, I didn't have to wait long because a friend of mine needed a favor.

My friend's dad was about to retire, and he wanted to do something to mark the occasion. Since his dad had been an automotive engineer and loved classic cars, he asked if I

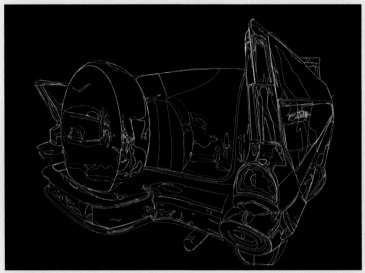

'57 Chevy, Process 1: Tracing by hand and scanning the reference image.

Since I hadn't had the chance to buy a digitizing tablet yet, I had to trace the image by hand first. Though it was tedious and time-consuming, Vincent rightly pointed out that it was much easier to break down the objects that make up an image with pencil and paper.

Once I had the photograph traced, I scanned it into the computer and used it as a background to build my objects in the vector program. As I had done with the camera, the smaller shapes came first, then the larger ones.

"Now that you've got your basic outline, why don't you start working on the right side of the car?" Vincent suggested.

"I think I want this to look a bit more like an illustration than the camera," I said. "The camera had to look almost like a photograph. I want this image to appear somewhere in between."

"Then you should be very loose in building your objects. You don't have to be highly structured in your shapes" Vincent said. "You might think your objects should be closer to the original tracing, and you could build the objects tighter if you

wanted to. But when you step back from your image, you'll see that those loose objects remain true to the shapes and textures of the car. It gives you that illusion of realism."

With the smaller objects completed, I then defined the larger shapes on the right side of the car, putting them in the background.

As I continued on to the right tail fin, I noticed there weren't many larger shapes to define it; most of them were very small.

"I'm not really sure how to approach the chrome," I said to Vincent. "I didn't have to do any chrome for the camera."

"Think of the water drops we did for 'Vision,'" Vincent sug-

"Now that you've got your basic outline, why don't you start working on the right side of the car?"

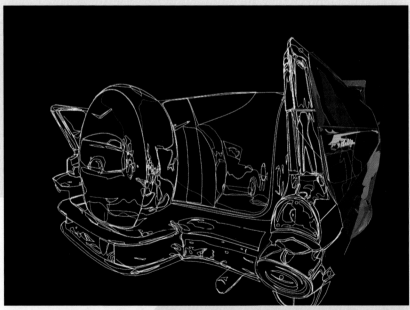

'57 Chevy, Process 2: Building objects and detail with the intent of realism.

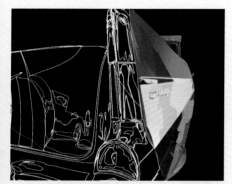

'57 Chevy, Process 3: Defining smaller objects first, then larger areas.

gested. "Those were abstract shapes. The way chrome reflects light is the same way. Just draw some shapes within the chrome areas. You don't need any real thought process to them; just follow what you see in the photo."

"And it will look right?" I remained a bit skeptical.

"You can't really go wrong with chrome," Vincent assured me. "Just about any shape you build within the chrome will work."

It was fun to simply create some abstract shapes on the chrome of the car's tail fin. And Vincent was right. Even though the shapes had no logic to them, the resulting image worked. I grouped together the objects that made up the car's right side and tail fin and hid them.

To make the image just a little more interesting, I had also photographed an antique, 1920s vintage car, traced its image, and placed it as a reflection off the '57

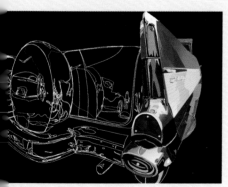

'57 Chevy, Process 4: Working on chrome.

Chevy's spare tire and trunk. As I moved to this section, I again started with the smaller objects, which were mostly made up of reflections.

"Your reflections should be a darker color than the actual trunk color," Vincent noted. "And you'll want those shapes to be even looser."

"And I'll still be able to make out what those shapes are supposed to be?" I asked.

"Sure," Vincent replied. "Remember, you want this to be a little abstract. Even as basic as those shapes are, you'll be able to tell that there's another car in there and possibly some people in the reflection."

'57 Chevy, Process 5: Adding color, reflections to trunk area.

Having completed the various shapes for the trunk lid — and observing that Vincent had been right about the reflections — I layered the larger objects behind the others.

'57 Chevy, Process 6: Adding gradient color to layered objects.

"I think we need some kind of gradient to create the right lighting effect," I said. "What do you think?"

"Why don't you try making a couple of gradients with a bit of overlap," Vincent suggested. "I think it looks more realistic that way."

Creating the gradients was almost second nature for me now. But when I finished, I noticed that the edges didn't quite match up.

"I've had this problem before with my previous images," I remarked. "Should I try to fill in those gaps with polygons like I did in 'The Camera,' or wait until I bring the image over to the raster program like I did with 'Vision'?" I asked.

"Why don't you save it for raster?"

Creating

the gradients was

almost second nature

for me now.

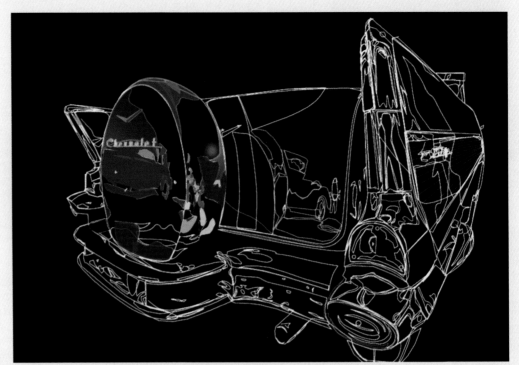

As I had done in the past, I hid the objects from the trunk lid and went to work on the spare tire, which Vincent informed me was known as a Continental kit.

'57 Chevy, Process 7: Working with the Continental kit.

"I know I've been making the objects very loose, particularly on the chrome," I noted. "But for the lettering that spells out 'Chevrolet,' don't I need to make the objects tighter so the letters are readable?"

"Not really," Vincent replied. "It's a basic shape, and you don't need a lot of detail. Even if it isn't a tight rendering of what the nameplate looks like, you'll still be able to tell what it is."

Like the "Chevrolet" badge, the rest of the shapes on the Continental kit were very small, free, and loose.

Now that the smaller shapes on the Continental kit were complete, I built the two larger shapes, added color, and ranked them in the background. Then, I grouped all the objects and hid them.

At Vincent's suggestion, my next step was the car's bumper. Again, it was a process of building smaller, then larger shapes. I then ranked the larger shapes behind the smaller ones.

By now, the only objects left to build were in the left tail fin. This one was much easier than the right tail fin because it mostly contained smaller shapes, and only a few of them at that.

Up to now, I had been hiding each segment of the

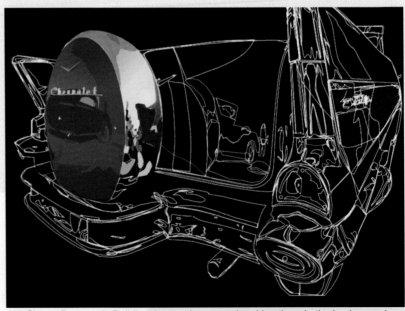

'57 Chevy, Process 8: Building larger shapes and ranking them in the background.

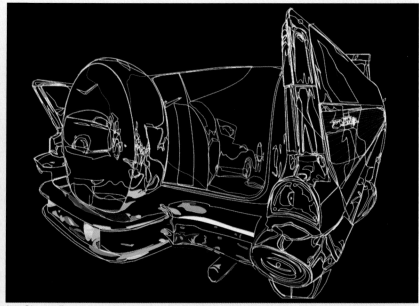

'57 Chevy, Process 9: Working on the bumper.

car as I completed it. Now it was time to un-hide everything before taking the image over to the raster program.

"I'm almost afraid to look," I confessed to Vincent. "I know the individual segments look good, but I don't know how it will all look together."

Vincent just gave me a serene smile as I un-hid the objects. Then he grinned.

"See? You didn't have anything to worry about," he said. "It looks great."

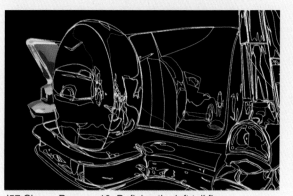

'57 Chevy, Process 10: Defining the left tail fin.

"We could almost stop right here," I began, "But..."

"But, we'll make it even better after we take it into raster," Vincent assured me. "The main thing we'll do there get rid of some of the edges."

I had already launched the raster program and opened up my saved file. "I do want to keep some of those hard edges, particularly in the chrome," I said.

"That's fine. But there are some places where you want to soften the edges, like with those two gradients on the trunk lid," Vincent replied. "You can create some highlights, and also create a bit of the ground texture that would be picked up in the reflections."

'57 Chevy, Process 11: All the objects un-hidden, the image is ready for the fine-tuning of a raster program.

Now it was time to un-hide everything before taking the image over to the raster program.

'57 Chevy, Process 12: Creating texture and highlights.

"Maybe we can add some textures from the ground off the right side of the car and the right tail fin," I suggested, clicking on the airbrush tool and selecting a darker brown color.

"Good idea," Vincent said. "Add some variations to the color, create a bit of a curve to show that it's been reflected, and darken some of the areas."

With the simple airbrush tool, I picked up some texture for the dirt that would have been reflecting onto the car. I also blurred some of the edges in the chrome areas, adding a few more colors and swirls inside the chrome itself, again using the airbrush.

"I really like how this image is shaping up," I said as I finished blurring the edges that I wanted to soften. "But I want to be sure it's the best I can do. Can you think of any detail I might have missed?"

Vincent looked at the screen for a minute or two. "You've got some nice lighting effects," he said. "But chrome is especially reflective. What if you added a sunburst to the chrome on the Continental kit?"

"That's it!" I exclaimed. "I knew I was missing something!"

Going back to my airbrush tool, I selected yellow and laid down a small highlight on the chrome band sur-

rounding the Continental kit. Then with my polygon tool, I created some rays, filling them with a transparent yellow.

"It's the little touches that can really make the difference in an image," Vincent observed when I was done. "This is going to make a great retirement gift for your friend's dad."

"And I think it will look pretty sharp on my wall, too." A few months had passed since I first entered the old warehouse and met my future through an abandoned computer. Thanks to Vincent's expertise, opinion, and infinite patience, I had gradually learned how to create my art on the computer.

With Vincent's help, I had created a number of images, including Vision, The Camera, and '57 Chevy. Each had special significance; Vision because it was my first real attempt to create computer art; The Camera because it was my first commercial computer image; and the '57 Chevy simply because it turned out so well.

There were other projects, some more successful than others. Each image that we created was a learning experience; Vincent constantly pushed me to stretch my abilities. I tried just about every tool both the raster and vector programs had to offer —

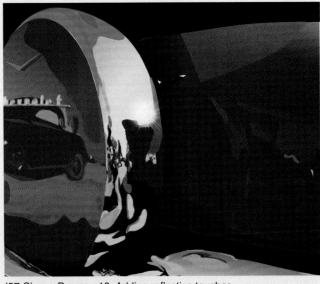

'57 Chevy, Process 13: Adding reflective touches.

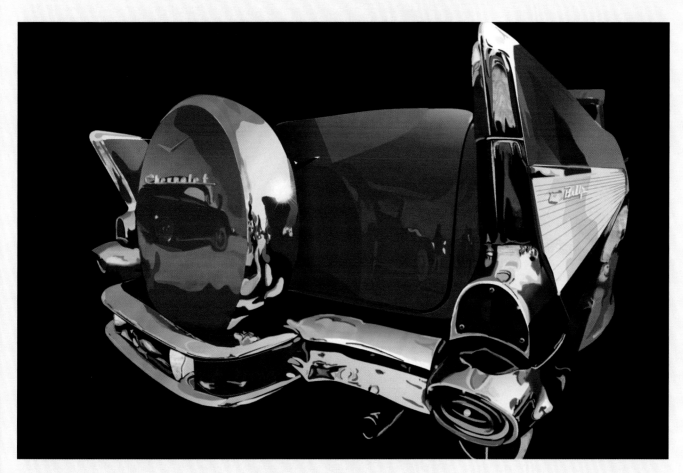

building, blurring, shaping, colorizing, interpolating, airbrushing — exploring the power of the computer to create art.

It wasn't easy. Many times, it took several attempts and techniques to achieve the look I wanted. On several occasions, I overtaxed my computer, either slowing it to a crawl or locking it up completely. And there were times when I just had to shut down the computer and walk away for a while.

The satisfaction in creating a powerful image, however, easily overshadowed the difficulties involved. The capabilities of the computer and the vast array of tools at my disposal continued to amaze me.

Though I would still use traditional art tools for some projects, the computer had radically transformed my art — and my life.

Of course, none of this could have happened without Vincent. He had done so much more than just show me how to generate computer graphics. By explaining the history of the medium and the inner workings of the computer, he placed my work in context. And by going through the fundamentals of computer art before I even began, he gave me a solid foundation from which to create.

Through my first series of images — including the three presented in detail — Vincent explained how

best to realize my ideas step-by-step. He suggested techniques, answered my questions, and critiqued my work. All of which helped me grow and gain greater confidence at the computer.

Gradually, I became less dependent on Vincent. I always had him around when I created my images, but I tried things on my own initiative. And he gave me the freedom to experiment and learn from my mistakes. Our relationship evolved from that of a student and teacher to an artist and mentor.

One day, I decided it was time to truly express my gratitude to Vincent in the best way I knew how — through my art.

"Vincent," I said, "I want to make a picture for you."

Vincent looked surprised and pleased at the same time. "Really?"

"Yeah. I've been thinking about it for a while now, and I can picture what I want in my head," I replied. "It's kind of a composite of everything you've taught me, a representation of what that has meant to my work — and to me."

Vincent was beaming now. "I would be honored," he said. "I just have one favor to ask."

"Name it."

"I'd like to watch you create it."

"But if you stick around, I'll end up asking for your advice." I protested.

"I'll leave you alone," Vincent promised. "For me, the greatest joy will be watching you create — and seeing the principles I've instilled in you at work."

"All right then, you can stay," I relented. "I don't mind if you ask about what I'm doing. But please, let me do this on my own as much as possible."

The Artist Will Simply Create: Detail of completed image.

As I began my image, the first thing I did was go to my art table, where I had my watercolors.

"I don't mean to butt in so soon," Vincent said. "But I can't really see what you're doing over there."

"Oh, I'm brushing out some shapes with my watercolors," I replied as I worked. "One of the

The Artist Will Simply Create, Process 1: Scannin hand-done watercolor.

first things you taught me was there are some things better left to traditional media. I wanted to include something like that in the image, and besides, watercolors produce some interesting, organic forms."

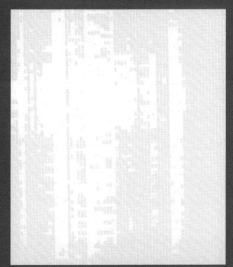

The Artist Will Simply Create, Process 2: Copying and enlarging to the point of distortion.

"That's true. Watercolors do some interesting things that you might not expect," Vincent said.

I held up some different watercolor shapes. "Is there one you prefer?" I asked.

Vincent studied the shapes for a minute. "I rather like that one on the right," he said. "It's got a bit of a flourish to it."

"Then that's the one I'll use," I said as I placed in the scanner to scan into a raster-based program on the computer.

"You'll have to excuse me for a minute," I told Vincent, "but I have to use the copier for the next part of this image."

"Why?" It felt a little odd for Vincent to be asking me questions.

"I have this picture," I explained, "and I'm just going to keep blowing it up on the copier until it becomes distorted. Then, I'll scan that into the computer, too."

Now, it was time to go back to the computer. Bringing up the image from Process 2, I decided to change its black pixel values to a new color.

"I know there are a few ways to change the color values," I said. "Wouldn't you say the seed fill tool would work best here?"

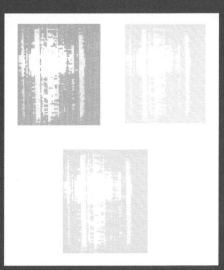

The Artist Will Simply Create, Process 2A: Usiing the fill tool to add color to 3 versions of the image in Process 2.

Vincent nodded. "As long as the program you're using has it; not all of them do," he said.

Fortunately, my program did. The seed fill tool located the edges of the pixels according to the variables that I had set. Then, I filled the pixels with the color I wanted.

"I think I'll try this image in a couple of different colors," I said as I saved the file under a new name. Using the same seed tool technique, I saved three versions of

The Artist Will Simply Create, Process 3: Compositing the colored images over the watercolor.

Process 2 in shades of purple, orange, and green.

"Now I'm going to combine the images," I explained as I brought up Process 1 on the screen.

Since Process 1 is black on a white background, I selected color values for the black pixels to be completely transparent and the white ones opaque. For my three versions for Process 2A, I made the white pixels completely transparent, and the color values I had assigned opaque.

"When I composite the three colored images over my watercolor, I'm offsetting each one slightly," I explained. "I think it creates a cool effect, with bits of all the colors throughout."

"I like the texture you've achieved," Vincent said. "It's very abstract, very intriguing."

"Thank you. I'm not sure how I would have done it without the computer."

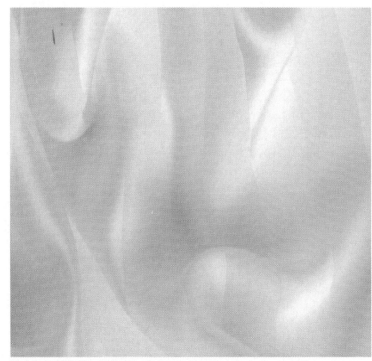

The Artist Will Simply Create, Process 4: Adding the texture of silk.

from red at the center to black at the outer edge.

"Since I'm already in the raster program, I'm using it to create my gradients," I explained. "I've found radial gradients tend to be much easier to do that way."

"Well, of course it's easy," Vincent said, laughing. "All you have to do is create a center gradient fill in."

I grinned back at him. "I know. Isn't technology great?"

With my radial gradients still on the screen, I brought in the silk image and composited it over the top of the gradients.

"What will make this image pop is that I'm selecting the black pixels

"I've noticed that there's no color inside the black areas," Vincent remarked. "If you took the image for Process 2 itself and laid it over the top of the image you created from it, there would be some value inside the black areas."

"What I did was select the white pixel value to be transparent in the Process 1 image," I explained. "That way, when I masked it over the top, the black area is opaque and knocks out any color inside the black area."

"A few weeks ago, I would have had to tell you to do that," Vincent said. "You're really applying the things you've learned."

"What do you think of silk?" I asked as I held up a picture before placing it in the scanner.

"It's beautiful to look at and has a nice texture," Vincent replied. "Another part of the image?"

"Yes, but I think it needs to be a bit bolder," I said. "I'll bump up the overall contrast to get deeper, darker shadows and more pure blacks."

"What about the color?"

"I'll change that, too," I said. Going into the image adjustment functions of the program, I changed the hue of the image to purple. "I know I could use the air-brush and paintbrush in the program to change the color, but this way is easier."

Opening a new file, I created some radial gradients, with the color changing

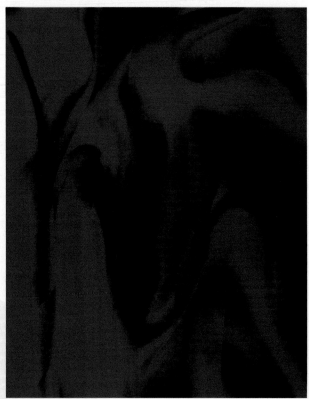

The Artist Will Simply Create, Process 5: Adding color to the texture with an image adjustment feature.

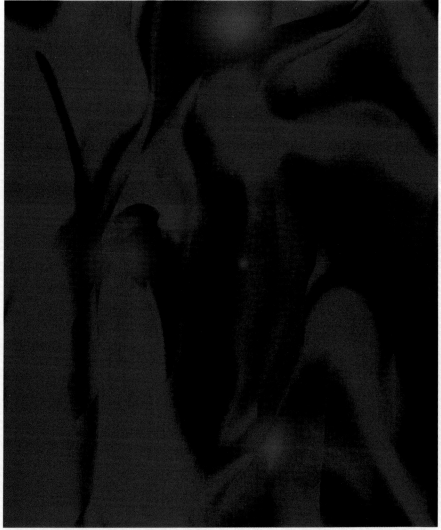

The Artist Will Simply Create, Process 7: The silk image composited over the radial gradients.

the watercolor and distortion over the top of the silk and gradients, I'm selecting the black color value to be transparent."

I could tell Vincent was becoming more excited as the image progressed. "I do like them better together," he said when I showed him the composite.

The Artist Will Simply Create, Process 8: More composites of the layers of images.

from the silk image to be transparent," I said. "Since some of the purple cuts through the spheres, it creates a real sense of depth."

"I like that last image — and the other composite, with the watercolor, too," Vincent remarked.

"You'll like them even better when I combine them." I said, completing the thought. When I composite

The Artist Will Simply Create, Process 6: Using radial gradients.

The Artist Will Simply Create, Process 9: Adding a degree of solidity to the image.

"No, I'll just save it in a file format that a raster program can open, and let it render the image for me."

To composite the interpolation onto the other composited imagery, I selected the black values in the file to be transparent. That way, the white lines would be composited onto the image.

"If you don't mind me saying so, you may need to balance the image out," Vincent pointed out. It's a little heavy on the left side."

I pretended to be annoyed. "I'm getting to that," I said. "I'll just add another black box, a little smaller this time, and still 50 percent black so you can see behind it."

"Now don't get all bent out of shape," I said warily as I held up another image to be scanned into the computer. "I just happened to have a copy of this sketch by da Vinci and wanted to include it in the image. If I had something by Van Gogh handy, I would have used it."

Vincent just laughed. "Why should I feel insulted?" he said. "Didn't I tell you? My middle name is Leonardo."

Still, I thought the composited image needed some solidity and weight. To break up the image somewhat, I created a rectangle on the left side and filled it with about 50 percent black. That way, it didn't completely block out the image underneath.

"Most of this image is being done in raster," I said as I closed the file and launched a vector program. "But I want to create a linear interpolation, which is much easier to do in vector."

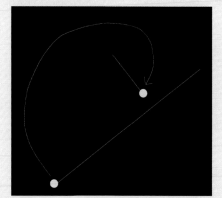

The Artist Will Simply Create, Process 10: Linear interpolation using a vector program.

Now it was my turn to laugh. "Good," I said. "Anyway, I'm going to scan this in using the high-contrast setting. That way, I'll get nothing but black and white pixels, which will make it easier to work with when I manipulate the image.

"So, you're going to create your own image

With that, I drew two different lines, the longer one to the right and below the other. I also drew the shorter line rotated to a different area.

"These are my selection points for the interpolation," I explained, pointing to two yellow balls on the screen. I selected my end points, with 55 objects to be interpolated between the two, and let the program create the interpolation.

"It looks sort of like an unraveling ball of twine," Vincent observed. "Are you going to render it into raster now?"

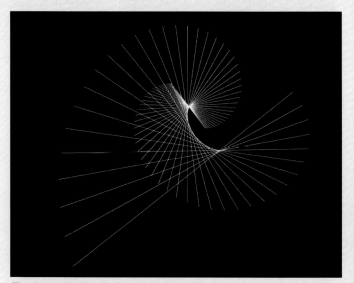

The Artist Will Simply Create, Process 11: Defining end points and objects.

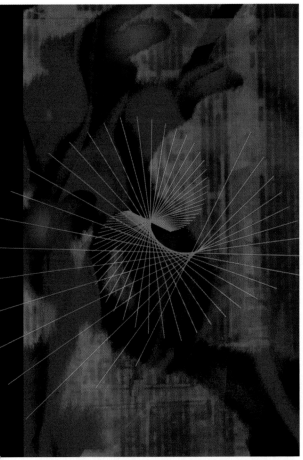

The Artist Will Simply Create, Process 12: Compositing the interpolation onto the composite imagery.

The Artist Will Simply Create, Process 13: Providing balance to the image.

based on Leonardo's genius?" Vincent raised his eyebrows.

I ignored the eyebrows. "Yes; to start with, I'll change the black pixels into orange," I said. "Now then, how do I want to do that?"

"You could use the image control functions to adjust the overall hue and value of a pixel according to its value at that given point," Vincent suggested. "That way, any changes you make only affect the black pixels and not the white ones.

"I guess I could do it that way," I said. "Or maybe I'll just use the seed fill tool. You're not supposed to tell me how to do this image, remember?"

"Sorry," Vincent said. "Once you become a teacher, you never really stop."

"Yeah, I know. I'm used to getting your advice, too," I replied. "But, the point is moot, because I'm not going to use any of those methods to work with Leonardo's sketch. I'm going to go into my vector program and trace over the top of the scanned image. That way, I can change the color values in those lines to whatever color I want, which in this case, is orange."

The Artist Will Simply Create, Process 14: A scanned image of a da Vinci sketch, used for reference.

"Now that you have Leonardo's sketch traced into the computer, what are you going to do with it?" Vincent asked.

"Well, first, I have to bring it into my raster program," I explained. "Then, I'm going to visually compress the image and place it over my black rectangle on the left. And when I composite it over the top of my other images, I'll make the background color transparent."

"Well, I don't know if that's what Leonardo would have done, but I like it," Vincent said.

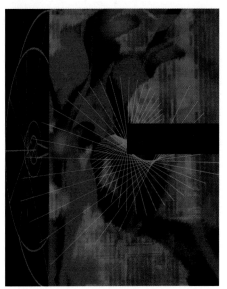

The Artist Will Simply Create, Process 15: Manipulating and compositing the image.

"Imagine what Leonardo could have produced if he had a computer," I replied.

"For the next part of the image, I may need your help," I told Vincent. "I want to create a very simple, three-dimensional shape to incorporate into the image."

"Well, except for that brief overview of the basics, we haven't done much in 3-D," Vincent reminded me. "It's an entirely different animal from the images you've created so far — a whole new set of lessons."

"Then I know what you'll be teaching me next," I said. "For this image, I just want a simple 3-D image, like a pair of rings. We've experimented with stuff like that before."

Vincent relented. "Okay, let's go back to the fundamentals of 3-D.

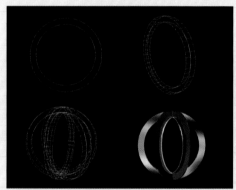

The Artist Will Simply Create, Process 16: A set of rings provides a simple 3-D image.

You need need to start with your most basic shape."

I drew two circles in the upper-left corner of the screen.

"Now, you need to extrude those lines along the z-axis," Vincent continued. "In some 3-D programs, you have to cut the hole out of the center."

"But in this program, if I extrude the circles at the same time, it creates the hole automatically," I said, placing the results of the extrusion in the upper-right corner.

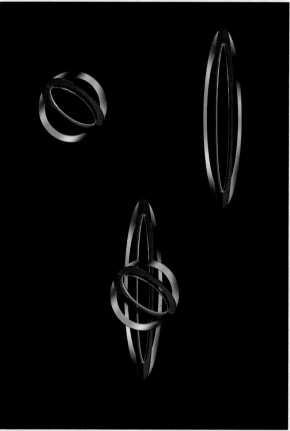

The Artist Will Simply Create, Process 17: Duplicating, rotating, and stretching to create a 3-D model.

"Do you know what to do next?" Vincent asked.

"If I duplicate this shape," I said, "I can rotate the new shapes along the y-axis, and center them on top of each other." I placed the duplicated and rotated shapes in the lower-left corner.

"Now what?"

"All I have to do now is add color and effects," I said, selecting one of the rings to be gold, another green, and the third a bright purple. When I was through, I pointed to the final shape in the lower-right corner of the screen.

"Not bad for an early effort," Vincent acknowledged. "I guess I'll have to prepare some more in-depth lessons on 3-D."

After I rendered my 3-D model into the raster program, I made a duplicate. Then, I stretched the copy along the y-axis and rotated it slightly, compositing the two rendered images together.

"We're almost through," I said as I brought up the previously composited images. Taking the composited 3-D image, I placed it over the top of the others.

"I really love it," Vincent said as he looked at all the images composited together.

The Artist Will Simply Create, Process 18: Adding the 3-D model to the previously composited images.

he **artist** will simply create

The Artist Will Simply Create, Process 19: Adding text to the finished image.

I could have typed the text in my vector program, brought it over to raster, made its background transparent, and composited it over the top of the image. But since my raster program could also generate type, I just typed what Stuart Preston had said, "the artist will simply create," in my raster program. Converting my typed text to an outline allowed me to fill in the shapes of the letters with color and outline.

After I finished enhancing the text, I got up from the computer so Vincent could see the final image.

Vincent peered thoughtfully at the screen. "The artist will simply create," he said quietly. "It kind of sums up what you've been doing lately, doesn't it?"

Then he burst into a wide smile. "It's magnificent," he said. "I must be one hell of a teacher."

"Yes, you are," I said with an equally big smile. "You've been both a teacher and an inspiration to me."

"Always happy to be of service," Vincent replied.

"So, where do we go from here?" I asked. "3-D?"

Vincent began to fade. "Maybe, but not today." He looked up at the darkened skylights. "Tonight, I mean. Why don't you get some sleep, and we'll tackle some new challenge tomorrow?"

I started to protest, still pumped with adrenaline from the creative process. But Vincent quickly faded away. I shut down the computer, turned out the lights, and went home.

"Hold on; there's one more thing I need to add," I interrupted him. "It's the finishing touch."

"What?"

"Well, back when you were explaining the history of computer art, you quoted an art critic from the *New York Times* who saw the computer's potential as an artist's tool," I said.

"Stuart Preston," Vincent interjected.

"Right. Well, I've really been inspired by what he wrote, and I want this image to reflect that."

c o m p

Art

Until The Camera—my first commercial computer art project—I had simply created images on the computer screen. All I had were soft copies, the digital files on my computer. But these were simple experiments with computer art, and except for Vision perhaps, I had no plans to hang copies on my studio walls.

For The Camera, however, I had to give my client a tangible, hard copy of the image, just as I had given clients production art of my conventional work in the past. Once again, I learned that the computer offers many options.

When my client first approached me about the job, I conferred with Vincent and made sure I could do it before committing to the project. One of the things Vincent and I talked about was output.

"First, you have to define how your image will be used," Vincent said. "Is it for advertising? Product

Out

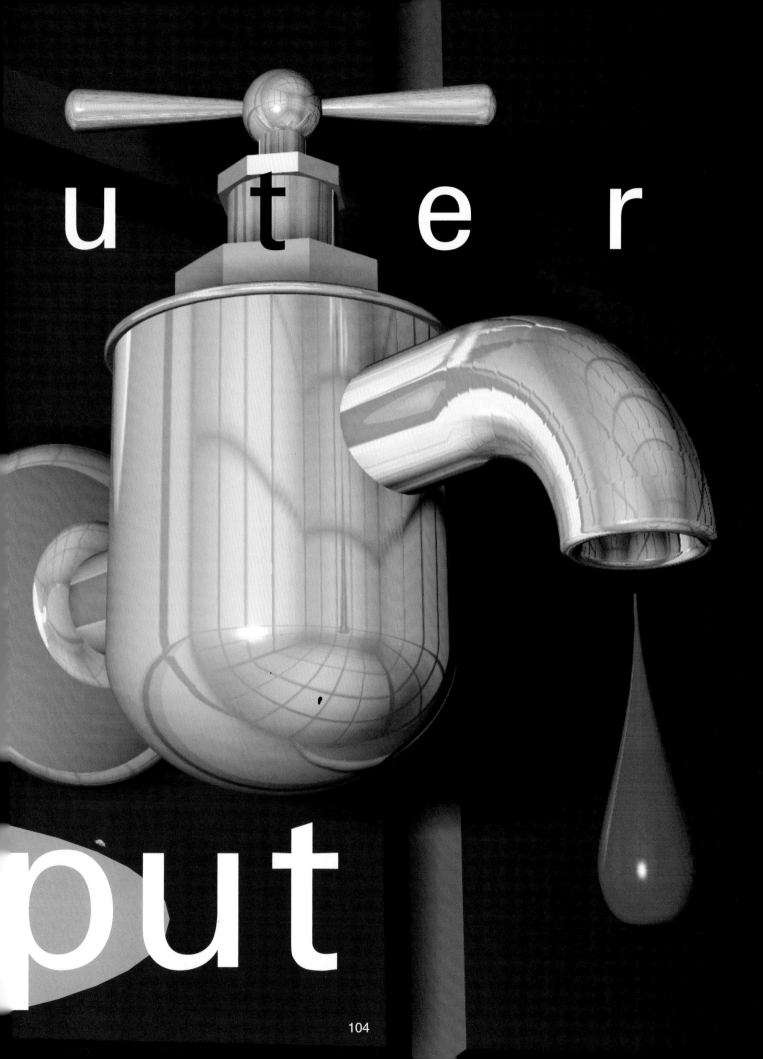

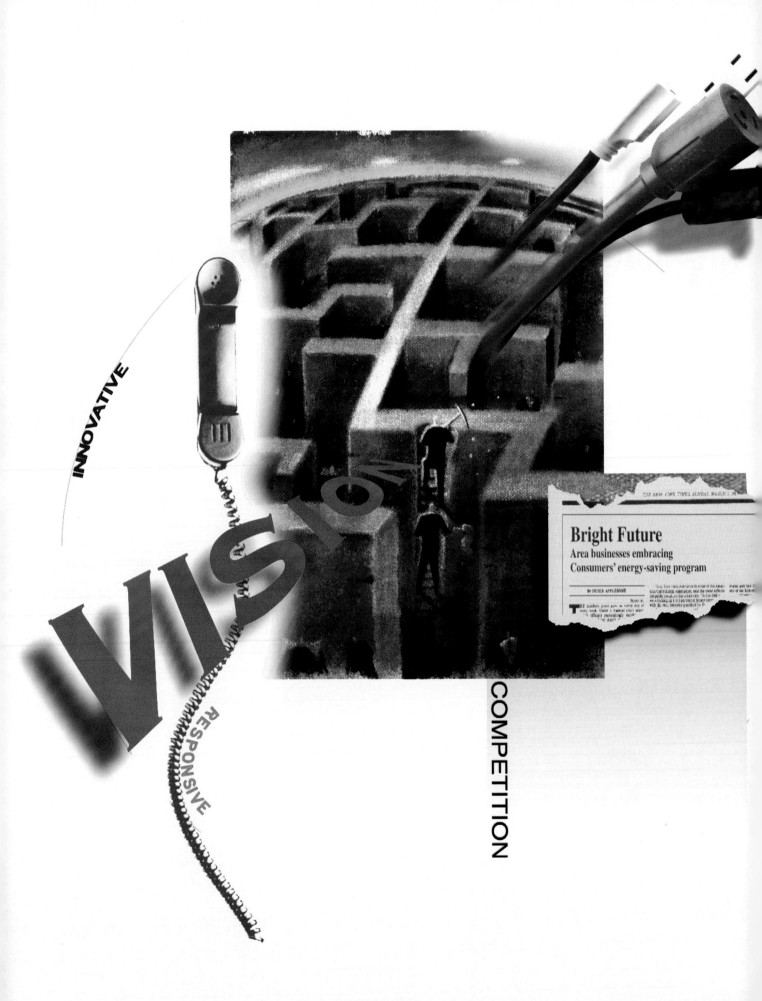

INNOVATIVE

VISION

RESPONSIVE

COMPETITION

THE NEW YORK TIMES, SUNDAY, MARCH 2, 20

Bright Future
Area businesses embracing
Consumers' energy-saving program

By PETER APPLEBOME

Do you need a large enough output for a display? How many copies of the image do they need? The answers will determine your output strategy."

"Well, I do know my client plans to use the image for an ad campaign and product literature," I replied. "And they're going to a trade show next month, so they'll need a display for their booth. Plus, I'd like to have a few copies of the image for my portfolio."

"All right, then, let's approach this systematically," Vincent began. "Knowing how you plan to use this image, I can recommend three distinct output strategies: digital printers, transparencies, and film separations for conventional printing processes."

"I take it there is a different purpose for each one?" I asked.

"Yes, and each has its own set of variables that affect your final output," Vincent said. "That's why I want to cover them separately."

"Why don't we start with the simplest option and work our way up?" I suggested.

"Okay," Vincent agreed, "that would be a digital printer connected directly to a computer."

"How is that different from my laser printer?"

"Well, the concept is the same, but color digital printers are specifically designed for color images," Vincent said. "There are several types on the market, including Iris printers, the Canon CLC 500 (also known as the Fiery), DuPont 4Cast, QMS, dye sublimation, and even low-end ink jet printers to name a few. Digital printers are computer-controlled and output your image directly from your image file."

"Which output would I use a digital printer for?" I asked.

"Your portfolio copies," Vincent replied. "Digital printers are a fast, economical way to print a limited number of copies. You wouldn't use one for the ads or literature because your client needs thousands of copies. It just doesn't make sense economically, particularly in terms of the dyes and inks these printers use."

"What about the trade show display?" I asked. "Is it too big?"

"Probably. Any printing device will be limited by the final page size it can output," Vincent replied. "Some printers can only print out 8.5x11 or 8.5x14 sheets; others can print larger pages."

"I could see using a digital printer to make proof copies or comps to show my clients," I said. "What about output quality?"

"That depends on several factors, but most digital printers are capable of high quality output," Vincent said. "Your file format, whether or not the printer output contains a dot pattern, and final output size are all variables to consider."

"When you say file format, do you mean raster or vector?"

Vincent nodded. "If you remember from our earlier discussions, a vector file is created from lines of code, whereas a raster file is created from individual pixels. The printer reads the code from a vector file directly, so it can output an image faster than it can a raster image."

"But I can still get high-quality output from a raster file, can't I?" I asked.

"Certainly; it all depends on the file resolution," Vincent said. "Remember, when you render a vector file over to raster, you can set your resolution to get the output quality you want. The higher you set your resolution, the more pixels your file contains, and the better output quality you'll get."

"What if I'm working entirely in raster with a scanned image?" I asked.

"The printer reads the code from a vector file directly, so it can output an image faster than it can a raster image."

"When you scan in the image, your scanning software will allow you to select an image resolution as well as other options related to image quality," Vincent replied. "Moving right along to the output variables, do you know what continuous tone is?" Vincent asked.

"Refresh my memory."

"A continuous tone image has no dot pattern to it whatsoever. If you look at a photograph, it has no dot pattern," Vincent explained. "If you look at an image on your monitor, you don't see a dot pattern. It's just one pixel after another. And there's no gap or space in between the pixels."

"And a digital printer can output to continuous tone?" I asked.

"Some can, yes," Vincent replied. "Some printers may only be able to output with a dot pattern. A small- or medium-size dot pattern will give you better quality output than a large dot pattern. And no dot pattern at all — continuous tone — will give you the best output."

"What about output size?"

"Go back to a previous discussion we had using an analogy with film formats. Remember, a photographer will use 4x5 inch film instead of 35 millimeter when he wants a higher quality image, particularly with a large final image size," Vincent explained. "In the same way, you will get a better output with a larger size output than you will with a smaller one.

"That takes care of outputting your portfolio copies," Vincent continued. "Now, let's take a look at your client's trade show booth display. As you correctly noted, it's too big to use a digital printer, so instead, we'll output it to a transparency."

"I've worked with photo transparencies before," I noted. "How would you get a computer file onto a transparency?"

"A device controlled by the computer images your file onto a transparency," Vincent replied. "In your client's case, you want to output to a transparency because of its large final output size. From the transparency, you can use a conventional photographic process to get your hard copy, which is either going to be a large reflective print, such as a duraflex, or a large transparent print, such as a duratrans."

"My client's booth display is going to be backlit, so wouldn't I need a duratrans?" I asked.

Vincent nodded. "Besides large prints, you would also want to output to a transparency if you have to separate the image for conventional printing or if you need a continuous tone image that will be separated in a different country where the standards are different," he said. "Transparency output is also used for slide presentations, and just like conventional photographs, you can make prints of a computer-generated image from a transparency."

"What are my variable issues?"

"A continuous tone image has no dot pattern to it whatsoever."

"In terms of input, they are the same as with digital printers: raster or vector; low-, medium-, or high-resolution," Vincent replied. "For output, it depends on the camera you're using to shoot the image and what resolution it can produce. You can choose from 2, 4, 8, or 16K for a low- to medium-quality image. For the best quality, there are cameras from Kodak and other high-end manufacturers."

"Why would you even consider output less than the highest quality?" I asked.

"It's a matter of cost," Vincent replied. "Cameras at the upper end of the scale tend to be more expensive. The difference in output quality may not always be enough to justify the expense."

"That's true," I acknowledged. "Since this is a photographic process, doesn't the size of my output also affect the quality?"

"Absolutely. You'll get a better output with a 4x5 transparency than you will with a 35mm," Vincent said. "And in the case of your client's trade show booth display, you'll want to go with an even larger 8x10 transparency. That way, when you blow the image up for the duratrans, it will still look good."

"That leaves us with the advertisements and product literature, which by process of elimination, will be conventionally printed," I said. "I've had my work printed before, but I don't know how I would prepare a computer-generated image for conventional printing."

"Why don't we start with a quick review of the printing process," Vincent said. "A conventional press uses a dot pattern photo-etched on plates that pick up the ink and lay it down on a page. And those plates are exposed from film taken of your image."

"Now, if I'm printing black and white, I only need a single piece of black film," I said. "And if it's a full-color piece, I'll need separations."

"That's right. Anything printed in full color has to be separated into four distinct colors: cyan, magenta, yellow, and black," Vincent explained. "Each color has its own separate sheet of film, from which metal plates are made to put on the press. The four colors are then printed

on top of each other, which produces the original image — or the closest available approximation — on the page."

"The four-color printing process I understand," I said. "How do I separate my image files and what variables affect my output quality?

"Making the separations themselves is nothing difficult; one method is having a service bureau output separations from your digital files," Vincent replied. "Most of your image quality considerations — raster, vector, resolution, and output size — are the same as for your other output methods. One thing to remember, though, your image has to be screened in order to print it on a conventional press. In fact, this is the only time your image has to have a dot pattern. You cannot re-screen an image. So if you use a digital printer that produces a dot pattern, or any other method of output that creates a screen, you cannot use that output for conventional printing."

"The unique variable to consider with separations is the line screen of your image," Vincent continued. "Line screen refers to the number of dots per linear inch. The smaller and more numerous the dots, the finer your line screen and the cleaner your image will appear when you output it," Vincent explained. "An image that is output at a 150-line screen contains 150 dots per linear inch. That's medium-level quality. A line screen of 30-125 is low-quality, while high-quality output requires a 180-600-line screen.

"So all I have to do is set the line screen for my file at 150 if that's the output I want?"

"No. If you're printing your film at a 150-line screen, the digital file of your image needs to have 300 pixels per inch to print correctly," Vincent said. "Some programs may refer to this as dots per inch, even though it's pixels. The output device needs twice the number of pixels for the specified line screen to create the film correctly."

"Why the difference in line screen between the film output and the digital file?"

"It's a simple formula. The dots per inch — or the amount of information/pixels per inch — should be double what the line screen is going to be," Vincent said. "The whole issue has to do with how much information is in the file to make it output correctly."

"But what if I can't output to screen film for printing?" I said. "What are my alternatives?"

"You could output one continuous-tone hard copy of the image using one of the printers we talked about earlier, or you could output to a transparency," Vincent explained. "Then you can scan and separate the image from there. Ideally, however, you want to work with the original digital file. It's the best way to go to maintain the quality of your image."

"Is there anything else I need to know about output?"

"Well, I haven't covered the entire printing process," Vincent replied. "But now you know your major output options and the variables you have to consider."

"I also know how I'm going to output the image," I observed. "Now all I have to do is create it."

"Which I'll help you on," Vincent pointed out.

"Well then, let's put the quote together for my client so that we can get started."

Profiles of computer Artists

Computer art, I discovered, is a continuously evolving process. So, in addition to the art and other magazines I had always read, I began looking at some of the computer art publications and design books. I wanted to see what other computer artists were doing and learn about new hardware, software, and techniques. I also found looking at different images helped stimulate ideas in my own mind.

As I read, I came across several artists whose work really interested me. And since I was still developing my own style as a computer artist, I decided to talk to these artists, find out how they began, what they're currently working on, and how they approach the creative challenges of computer art. Each turned out to have experiences as unique as his art.

Mark Jasin

I reached Mark Jasin on a cold, snowing day at his Denver studio, where, besides trying to keep warm, he was busy working on several projects. Thanks to the computer, he has the power and flexibility to create unique, original artwork within the tight deadlines of his clients.

"The computer has absolutely expanded my creativity," Mark said. "I have a bank of personal

imagery that I created; it's like my own personal clip art. I can take an image, rearrange it, or in some way make it reusable for another project and still make it look original."

Mark said he doesn't try to create art that necessarily looks like it was produced on the computer. In fact, he would do the same kinds of images even if he wasn't using the computer. But the kinds of art Mark prefers — graphic illustration and photo manipulation — "are those that the computer does best."

As a dynamic tool, the computer allows Mark to preview work before it goes to separations or any proofing stages, giving him multiple choices for layouts, images, and colors. Also, he can deliver very tight finished comps — which his clients appreciate — and make more critical judgments in terms of final output.

When Mark graduated from Arizona State University in 1991, he had a degree in graphic design, but no computer experience. He had focused on illustration at ASU, and moved to Southern California to work on editorial illustrations for

GABRIEL'S

INTERFACE

WITH SOUTHWEST COLOR'S 8/8 MAC TECHNOLOGY FOR STATE OF THE ART POSTSCRIPT AND BITMAP FILM OUTPUT, CALL (713) 954-9941

ALDUS FREEHAND 2.02 ILLUSTRATION BY MARK JASIN, REPRESENTED BY MARTHA PRODUCTIONS 213/204-1771

"I can take an image,

rearrange it, or in some way

make it reusable

for another project and

still make it look original."

the *Orange County Register*. The newspaper has a nationwide reputation for its informational graphics, art, and extensive use of four-color.

It was at the *Register* that Mark learned computer graphics on a very early version of Apple's Macintosh. There was no formal training, just hands-on experience. "You basically learned by trial and error," he said.

Because newspapers had an immediate use for computer graphics, they proved to be excelent training grounds for computer artists. Newspapers such as the *Register* also had the resources to invest in high-end technology before it became commonplace, so "I had a running knowledge of it before most people did," he said.

Once some of that high-end technology — such as 32-bit color — did become readily available, Mark decided to go out on his own. His first freelance project proved ideal for the computer.

Through the artist's representative he had hired, Mark got a job from the National Football League to generate helmet artwork for all 28 NFL teams. "They needed absolutely identical helmets for all the teams," he said. Previously, each helmet had been painted individually by hand, a difficult and expensive process, especially as teams made changes to their colors or logos. Using the computer, Mark could achieve the uniformity the NFL required, while making it much easier to change the artwork as necessary in the future.

In some of his other early jobs, Mark found he had to nurse his clients along at first, reassuring them that the computer art would look as good as they wanted and explaining the process to some degree. As his clients began using computers themselves and became more familiar with what

they could do, he found a greater acceptance for computer graphics, especially when clients learned of the time and cost savings over conventional artwork.

Mark's current client list includes several major companies. For Sprint, he's doing a job similar to his project for the NFL. A major sponsor for World Cup Soccer '94, Sprint has Mark creating long-distance calling cards with specific designs for each of the 24 participating teams. He's also working on projects for Miller Lite's Pro-Beach Volleyball Tour and trade advertising illustrations for Motorola, among others.

All Mark's work comes through his rep. "I prefer it that way. I prefer her to do all the business, all the negotiations, and from there I do everything else." And although he wouldn't try to freelance without one, he doesn't think having a rep is absolutely

There was no formal training,

just hands-on experience.

"You basically learned

by trial and error," he said.

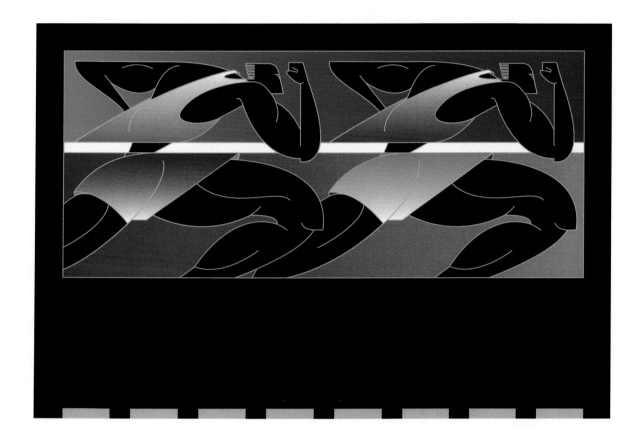

necessary. It is, however, a good idea for people who don't want to bother with the business end of commercial art, he said.

Mark's equipment has come a long way from the early Macintosh he used at the *Register*. He uses a Mac Quadra 950 with 102MB of RAM, and three external hard drives. That way, he said, you don't lose the entire computer if a drive goes down. He also has a 19-inch, 32-bit color monitor, a slide scanner and a flatbed color/black & white scanner, a 32bis modem, accelerator cards, and a video card accelerator for the Quadra.

Mark uses Aldus FreeHand for EPS drawings and Adobe Photoshop for image manipulation, and his work is split roughly 50/50 between raster and vector images. For output, he has a LaserWriter printer, and he might consider a color laser printer with dithering capability, depending on price. He's also interested in emerging technology for working with extra-large digital files, which would be especially important for fine art.

Mark said he uses the Mac because that's what he learned from the beginning, and for years it dominated the graphic arts field. Although IBM-compatible computers are catching up in graphics applications, Mark continues to believe "that for what we do in our field, the Mac is the stronger tool."

Regardless of the platform used or the technology that evolves, Mark believes the computer as an artist's tool is no fad. "This is a revolution that's permanent."

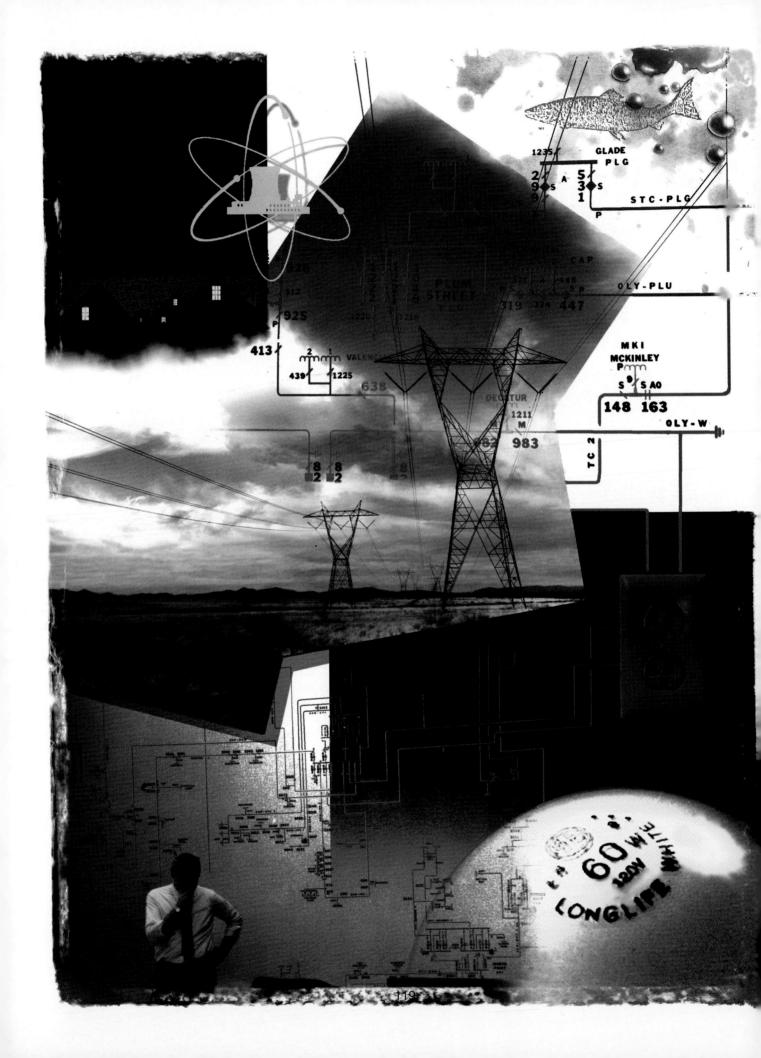

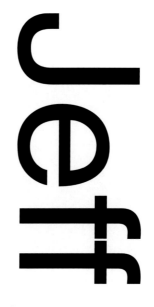

Jeff Brice

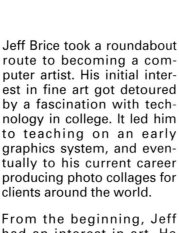

Jeff Brice took a roundabout route to becoming a computer artist. His initial interest in fine art got detoured by a fascination with technology in college. It led him to teaching on an early graphics system, and eventually to his current career producing photo collages for clients around the world.

From the beginning, Jeff had an interest in art. He said he always drew and painted growing up, especially landscapes. He continued to study art at the Parsons School of Design, and later Carnegie Mellon University in Pittsburgh, where he graduated with a Bachelor of Fine Arts in painting.

It was at Carnegie Mellon in 1978 that Jeff discovered technology as an artistic force. Video, a conceptual field of performance art, grabbed Jeff's attention. "I was fascinated by the technology of it," he said, enough so that he gradually moved away from painting and began working in video.

After graduation, Jeff left Pittsburgh for New York, where he got a fellowship at the New York Institute of Technology (NYIT), earning a Master's degree in communications. Jeff's emphasis at NYIT was television production, but he also taught in the art department, "so I had my feet in both worlds," he said.

In the early 1980s, NYIT developed IMAGES, a powerful computer graphics system based on mainframe computer technology that could be used in conjunction with television production. Jeff was asked to teach the system, and he "fell in love with the equipment. That's how I got into computer art," he said.

Having earned his master's degree, Jeff joined up with a New York airbrush artist to form a computer graphics company, Natale East, in

Out of that frustration, and his lack of money and space in New York to exhibit large paintings, Jeff experimented with simulation, creating a virtual gallery. "I simulated this whole series of work," he said, "I created this gallery on the computer with simulated paintings on a wall and created my own show out of them."

Although Jeff had learned computer art on a large mainframe computer, he saw the future in desktop graphics systems, and bought a Macintosh SE in 1987. Using such programs as MacPaint and Superpaint, he began experimenting, generating some silk-screen films. "It was freeing to be able to use my own computer," he said. "I had been using these huge computers for so long, and they were always tied to someone else. The idea of having my own computer, in my own home, even if it was limited, was just great."

Jeff left New York in 1988. With the client list for the IMAGES system in hand, he landed at Magicmation, a slide generation house in Seattle. "I knew they had one, and I figured I could get a job running it," he said. Magicmation's system wasn't even working at the time, but Jeff found that if he could get the IMAGES running, he had a job. It took two months.

While at Magicmation, Jeff worked with two other graphic artists who were forming a print division, using the Mac for print work, airbrushing, and combining images. With more powerful

1984. With access to NYIT's IMAGES system, Jeff could produce high-resolution illustrations, but he couldn't always get the desired output. And the IMAGES system was so expensive that it was difficult to make much money.

"We had a hard time," Jeff said. "No matter how much work we did, it would never even pay for the machine."

Two years after he left, Jeff went back to NYIT, again teaching in the computer graphics lab. The institute was then selling the IMAGES system commercially, and Jeff trained customers on it for a year. At the same time, he did some freelance and fine art work.

Jeff has created fine art throughout his career. "That's kind of been my inspiration," he said. At NYIT, he had access to the IMAGES system to produce his fine art, but output was still a problem. Despite experimenting with slides, silk screen, and other materials, "I was still frustrated by how to get the images on the wall," he said. "It always had to go to film, and I was never really satisfied with that."

Jeff has created fine art throughout his career. "That's kind of been my inspiration," he said.

software such as Color Studio and Photoshop, Jeff could do everything the IMAGES system did on a relatively inexpensive desktop computer.

Jeff went out on his own after a couple of years, buying a more powerful Mac system, and hiring a Seattle-based representative, Kolea Baker. He credits her with bringing in almost all of his work, and with a national client base, "She's taken my work and gotten it out there, and my whole career has taken off since then," he said.

Jeff's specialty is creating collages using photographs and computer generated imagery. Except for shooting photographs or painting textures, Jeff does everything on the computer. His creative process combines the methodical with the spontaneous.

Jeff said he hardly ever does sketches because a photo collage is very hard to draw out. Instead, he collects potential images, and all of his slides and graphic art are categorized by subject. When a job comes in, he sorts through potential images and begins planning how things might work together. Once he has selected the images, Jeff scans everything into the computer. And the spontaneity begins.

"I find that when I scan a photo in, I see things on the screen that I didn't see originally," Jeff said. "When I start combining them, they start reacting to each other. It tends to sort of create itself as it goes. I usually have some idea of what I want, but the more I let the process work itself, the better it's going to be."

Although Jeff said he begins a photo collage by just throwing things around to get it going, he's very particular about composition, and his images tighten up as he goes. "It's like working on a puzzle," he said. "I have to figure out how it's all going to work together."

As a creative tool, the computer has certainly influenced Jeff's work, he finds it exciting to be involved with technology as part of the creative process. At the same time, he isn't sure if the computer has enhanced his creativity. "I was creative to begin with, and then I was taught fine art." he said.

The computer has, however, pointed Jeff in different directions than he would have gone otherwise. With his continuing interest in photography, painting, and fine art, "the computer gives me that chance to work with all those things together."

Jeff spends about 90 percent of the time in working in raster programs such as Adobe Photoshop, Color Studio, and Specular Collage, with the remaining 10 percent in vector. His current system includes a Quadra 650 with 40MB of RAM, internal 1.5GB hard drive, external 550MB hard drive, internal CD-ROM, external Magneto Optical drive, a 44MB Syquest drive, and a Wacom tablet. He also has 19" and 13" monitors, a color scanner, and a color inkjet printer.

Several emerging technologies have attracted his interest, including live picture technology, and resolution independent software combining raster and vector. He's also interested in expanded use of fiber optics and interactive media.

Although Jeff doesn't need the computer to drive his creativity, he believes it does give more people the opportunity to express themselves. "The good thing about computer art is it's allowing all kinds of people to be creative who might not otherwise fit into the drawing, painting, and sculpture areas," he said. "There's lots of ways to be creative."

Although Jeff said

he begins a photo collage

by just throwing things around

to get it going,

he's very particular about composition.

brian Stauffer

Brian Stauffer never thought he would be doing what he is now — art direction for *New Times*, an alternative weekly newspaper in Miami. Even though his parents were both artists, and he grew up playing with their art supplies, he never thought of graphic art as a way to make a living.

"I probably thought I was going to work at Taco Bell," he said. "I didn't know what I was going to do."

So when Brian went to the University of Arizona in Tucson, he majored in music, classical saxophone and voice. But after practicing for hours and hours every day, "I decided that wasn't what I wanted to do," he said. "I turned around and went to the only other thing I felt comfortable with — actually much more comfortable with — and that was art."

Immediately, he knew he had done the right thing.

Perhaps unconsciously, Brian's upbringing had trained him to think visually. In early assignments with cut paper, Brian worked with how different shapes relate to each other and to the negative spaces. The fun part, he said, was when he had 4 to 5 different shapes of varying size, and he had to place them in a way that was both interesting and balanced with no restrictions or guides. "That was when it started to click as to what I was going to do," he said.

Brian didn't use a computer at all in college; his studies focused on the illustrative process, hand drawing, and silk screening. He said he was probably the last generation of art students at the U of A who weren't exposed to the computer as an artist's tool. As a result, he didn't know the computer offered unlimited creative possibilities, and he assumed it would only allow him to create a few special effects. "I thought I

annie

For a great segment of the American public, the internationally traveling exhibition, *Annie Leibovitz Photographs 1970-1990* should be more than familiar. Instantly recognizable, her images made for Rolling Stone, Vanity Fair and other publications have become famous for their particular character. Over time they have made up a vivid collective memory in American popular consciousness. The work of Leibovitz presently touring the country is a comprehensive survey of her career, with many surprises: elegant work done in Israel and the Philippines when she was still a teenager; less-known images of pivotal events such as Nixon's resignation, and numerous pictures previously unpublished. In large or small format, in color or black and white, Leibovitz covers a broad range of emotions and environments, from the stark isolation of an Edmund Muskie to the resilience of a Vaclav Havel.

leibovitz

by gary higgins

Mikhail Baryshnikov, 1990

Copyright Annie Leibovitz, 1991

$3.50

oct.–feb.

ZONE

7

ZON

philip glass

bob weir
peter shire
amy tan
the roches
lar lubovitch

william

burroughs

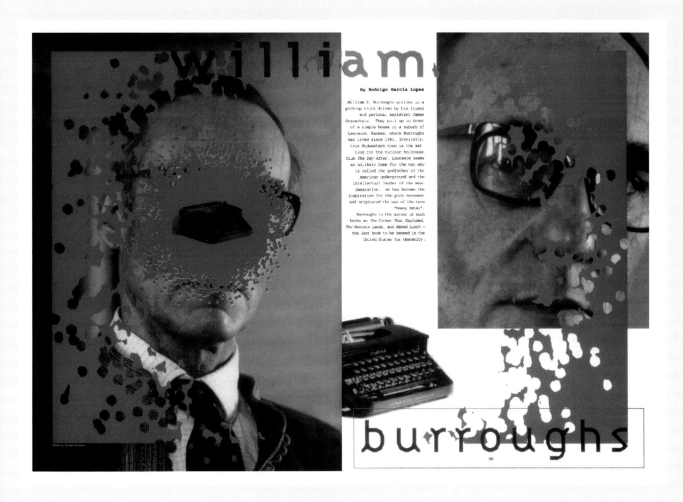

by Rodrigo Garcia Lopes

William S. Burroughs arrives in a pick-up truck driven by his friend and personal assistant James Grauerholz. They pull up in front of a simple house in a suburb of Lawrence, Kansas, where Burroughs has lived since 1981. Ironically, this Midwestern town is the setting for the nuclear holocaust film *The Day After*. Lawrence seems an unlikely home for the man who is called the godfather of the American underground and the intellectual leader of the Beat Generation. He has become the inspiration for the punk movement, and originated the use of the term "heavy metal".

Burroughs is the author of such books as *The Ticket That Exploded*, *The Western Lands*, and *Naked Lunch* — the last book to be banned in the United States for obscenity.

would end up fitting the design to what the computer could do as opposed to letting the computer pull the concepts out of my imagination," he said. "I had a tremendous bias against the computer because I was afraid of it."

Two years out of school, when Brian went to work for *Zone* magazine, he finally tried computer art out of necessity. "I had to learn the computer in order to do *Zone*," he said, but his biases didn't last long. "After sitting down at the computer for about two minutes, I realized I was wrong."

Once he began using the computer, Brian discovered he could

do the same kind of exploring he did in art classes with cut paper. In addition, the computer allowed him to "visually record" his ideas, giving him multiple shapes and combinations in a fraction of the time. He said the ability to move elements around and see the results opened his mind to possibilities he wouldn't have thought of otherwise.

Brian found his niche in magazine page layout at *Zone*, where he is now a part-owner and self-titled design guy. He has a

couple of people who do some of the page layouts and with whom he can bounce ideas around, "but for the most part, that's my baby," he said.

As art director for *New Times*, he is bringing a new level of graphic intensity to serious editorial subjects such as international

"The limitations

to your creativity are extinct," he said.

"That's unsettling.

You don't have any more excuses."

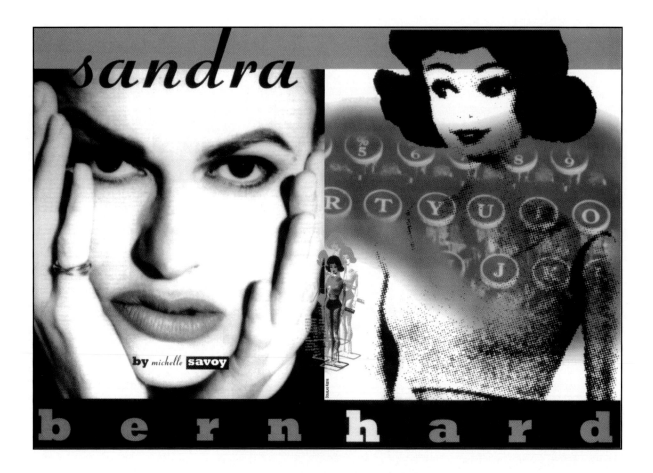

sandra

by michelle **savoy**

bernhard

drug smuggling rings. He said it's probably one of the first times post-modern graphic design has been applied to such weighty topics. The designs attract people who wouldn't ordinarily read such stories.

Brian currently uses a Mac IIci with 8MB of RAM and a 200MB hard drive, a color monitor, and a high-resolution color/gray scale scanner. He said he will probably upgrade to Macintosh Quadra with a CD-ROM drive, after which he plans to convert his vintage photo library to CD-ROM. Most of his work is typographic, so the programs he uses the most are Quark XPress, Adobe Illustrator, and Aldus FreeHand.

Brian believes the computer has definitely influenced his work. Without the computer,

he said the elements on the page would be less dynamic and the designs less surprising because "it's a lot easier to get into the same thing," he said. And he wouldn't have the time to explore multiple ideas for a project, then combine elements for all of them.

"The computer allows me to go completely crazy and do whatever I want," he said. Often, I'll go back to the foundation within a layout and reapply something I've come up with during all the experimentation. I do it in the computer because I know I'm not eliminating any possibilities."

Because computer artists can experiment so readily, Brian believes they shouldn't feel limited to or comfortable with a particular style. "It's important that what I do is not just

regurgitated stuff," he said. Page layouts from *Zone*, for instance, may look like they were created by different people, even though he did all of them. The style of these designs, he said, was driven by their content.

Looking back, Brian believes the lack of a formal education in computer art may have been a blessing. His more traditional training in art, he said, taught him to think visually and freely associate words and images.

Still, the computer has arrived as an artistic force, and he believes artists who continue to avoid it have to overcome their fears. "People need to make an informed decision about computers," he said.

"They are doing themselves no favor by making a decision about technology without having looked into it and giving it some consideration."

More important than the fear of technology, however, is an issue that Brian — as well as other computer artists — must face: the unlimited possibilities available with the computer.

"It's an intense fear because you're facing something you never expected to in your life: that the limitations to your creativity are extinct," he said. "That's unsettling. You don't have any more excuses."

Ron

For Ron Scott, photography started out as a hobby. Then, it became a career. And finally, it took him into 3-D imagery and developing photo manipulation software.

When Ron was at Tulane University in New Orleans in the mid 1960s, he studied physics and mathematics. He had gotten interested in photography while growing up, and at Tulane, he turned his hobby into a job with the school newspaper and yearbook. He spent his first years after graduation working for a general commercial photographer in Fort Worth. Then, when a friend from Tulane said he was moving to Houston, Ron joined him to open a photo studio in 1970. About two years later, he went out on his own.

By the early 1980s, Ron became aware of how the computer would affect photography in the future. He believed the computer was just another way to produce images; like the camera, it was a high-tech tool for making pictures. "The concept fascinated me because you could completely create the image with a machine," he said. "I thought it gave a rather unique look to the images."

Ron investigated what systems were available, but at the time, most com-puter-based imagery was limited to Computer Aided Design/Computer Aided Manufacturing (CAD/CAM). He finally bought Cubicomp, the first system for 3-D modeling on the IBM personal computer. "I simply jumped in at the first opportunity I saw to buy something that could produce things that looked like pictures as opposed to things that looked like CAD/CAM or line drawings," he said.

Scott

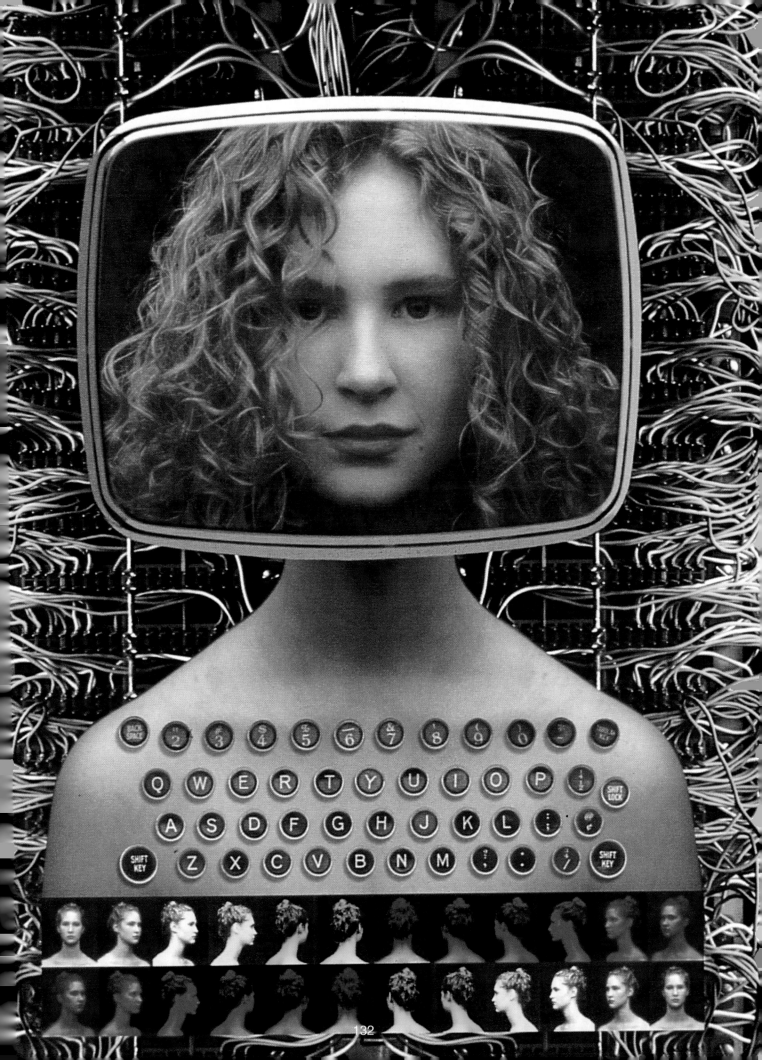

Although Cubicomp allowed Ron to create 3-D images complete with lighting, shading, and shadows, the technology was still extremely limited. There were no scanners available, nor were there any film output devices or output options beyond video.

Because of those limitations, Ron decided to develop his own "fairly crude, but highly effective" image editing software. With it, he could use the video screen as a bird's eye view of the image. He could also pull sections of the image into the video graphics system and edit it in the video frame buffer, then paste it back into the main image.

Ron's Cubicomp system did not have true color capabilities. It was color mapped, and then it offered just 16-bit color. However, as Targa boards and 24-bit color became available in the mid-1980s, Ron could use it and the accompanying TIPS paint program to edit any size image. "This made it fairly easy for me to edit and do photo retouching on high-resolution images," he said.

Although most applications for color seemed to be targeted toward the video market, Ron saw the potential for desktop color image editing. So, from the earlier programs he had written, Ron developed QFX and HiRes QFX,

designed specifically for systems such as his with limited amounts of RAM — 1MB expandable to 2-3MB. "All along, the idea was to allow myself and others to be able to edit high-resolution images on rather modest systems," he said.

Ron's work in software development includes some of the early concepts for the alpha channel through his work with Cubicomp. He said his dad, a scientist, mathematician, and inventor, first proposed the idea of an alpha channel, "even though we didn't call it that." The goal

was to create a soft-edged mask, a previously impossible feat. "I spent years working with all kinds of products trying to achieve something that's totally opaque in one area and totally clear in another and yet has a smooth gradation between the two," he said.

Ron and his dad realized early on that because computers work in bits and bytes, there would eventually be 32-bit computers. They also believed that 24 bits, a combination of eight bits of red, green, and blue, would probably be enough for most images. That left an extra 8 bits, "and my dad said you ought to do something with that extra memory," Ron said.

All along, the idea was

to allow myself and

others to be able to edit

high-resolution images

on rather modest systems," he said.

At the 1983 SIGGRAPH conference, two programmers from Lucasfilm, who had been advisors on the early Cubicomp system, presented "Compositing Digital Images," a technical paper that codified how the alpha channel would work and what it would do.

It took some time for the alpha channel to catch on, however. "Whenever we said alpha channel, it threw the technophobes into convulsions," Ron said. As with other innovative concepts, a lot of people dismissed the idea or shied away from it, labeling the alpha channel "too difficult to use or too far out. Then, of course, once it becomes accepted, it turns out you were a visionary."

Although Ron was spending more of his time developing software by the mid-1980s, he did produce several images for commercial projects. One of the first was for SIGGRAPH '86. He had been doing a lot of photo work for a Dallas design firm, which knowing he was involved with computer graphics, offered Ron the chance to create the conference poster.

What they didn't know was that Ron was working on a 286 PC. The members of the SIGGRAPH committee, who were used to their powerful DEC systems, couldn't believe he could actually create an image on a lowly PC. But they stuck with me, he said. After that, he did a magazine, book covers, some advertising, and a lot of annual report covers. With limitations of the hardware, however, it took so long to create some of these images his clients couldn't justify the cost.

"I used to caution my clients that the fact I was doing it on the computer did not make it cheaper and faster, which is of course, what got into the minds of the public early on," he said. "You have to be very careful about the naive assumptions that you make."

Even though today's computer technology has eliminated such limitations, Ron devotes almost all of his time to software development. He does create images occasionally "to keep my hand in it," as well as for software demonstrations and the occasional assignment.

Naturally, Ron uses his HiRes QFX software when he creates images. His hardware includes a Dell 486 PC with 80MB of RAM, a 500MB hard drive, Targa board, and a Super VGA card on the motherboard. Another graphics program he uses is TIPS, which may be old by computer standards, "but it's easy to use and straightforward," he said.

Ron has maintained his interest in photography throughout the technological accomplishments he has witnessed in his career. "This digital revolution is having a profound effect on photographers," he said, and there are several emerging technological issues that photographers will have to address. One of these is whether images will be captured on film or electronically with digital cameras. The widespread availability of scanners and photo CDs brings up intellectual property issues, particularly for stock photography, he added.

Although computers have muscled into the photographer's turf, Ron doesn't believe they can replace the photographer's imagination. "Photography still is what happens in front of the camera," he said. "Whether the camera has a computer chip in it or film, it's still the photographer's job to isolate the image and determine what the image is, not simply take the picture."

As a commercial artist for several years, I already had some knowledge of copyright law, having copyrighted much of my work. However, creating art on the computer brought up several questions about copyright issues, particularly with the computer's capability to scan and manipulate images.

At Vincent's suggestion, I spent a day at the library researching some key copyright issues. He felt — and I agreed — that it would be valuable to have a clear understanding of copyright rules as I worked in computer art. He also suggested I summarize my findings so that I'd always have a reference handy.

Here's what I found:

A copyright is essentially a government's legal protection of a person's basic property rights — the exclusive right to the work of one's mind. The copy-

right owner of a work of art, literature, design, sculpture, music, or audio-visual presentation possesses the exclusive right to make copies of the work, to prepare derivative works from it, to sell it, license it, distribute it, or display it in public.

The basic concept at the foundation of copyright law is that if a person creates something and expresses it in a permanent form, that person owns it. The copyright laws are designed to provide legal protection against unauthorized and/or immoral usage, alteration, duplication, or sale of that work without the author's consent.

I am not purporting to give you specific legal advice. The copyright law is complex and detailed, and for advice on your particular situation, consult an attorney.

Legal Definitions of Copyright

As defined in the U.S. Constitution, Article 1, Section 8: "The Congress shall have the power... to promote the progress of science and useful arts, by securing for limited times to authors and inventors the exclusive right to their respective writings and discoveries."

Copyright is a form of protection provided by American law (Title 17, U.S. Code) to the authors of "original works of authorship," including literary, dramatic, musical, artistic, and certain other intellectual works, and is available to both published and unpublished works.

Section 106 of the Copyright Act generally gives the owner of copyright the exclusive right to do and to authorize others:

- To reproduce the copyrighted work.

- To prepare derivative works based upon the copyrighted work.

- To distribute copies of the copyrighted work to the public by sale or other transfer of ownership, or by rental, lease, or lending.

- To perform the copyrighted work publicly, in the case of literary, musical, dramatic, choreographed, or other audio-visual works.

- To display the copyrighted work in public, in the case of literary, musical, dramatic, choreographic, pictorial, graphic, or sculptural works, including the individual images of a motion picture or other audio-visual work.

The Berne Convention and Moral Rights

In 1989, the United States became the most recent country to accept this international doctrine. The Berne Convention established that certain inherent personal rights are afforded to creators of artistic works, even after the works have been sold or the copyright transferred.

These rights fall into four categories:

1. The right to protect the integrity of their work, to prevent any modification, distortion, or mutilation which would be prejudicial to their honor or reputation.

2. The right of attribution (or paternity) to insist that their authorship be properly acknowledged and to prevent use of their names for works they did not create.

3. The right of disclosure to decide if, when, and how a work is presented to the public.

4. The right of recall to withdraw, destroy, or disavow a work if it is changed or no longer represents their views.

While these are basic principles of "Berne" protection, Berne is not "self-executing." The extent to which these rights are protected in the U.S. depends on the specific application of various state and federal laws. However, a work must be registered with the U.S. Copyright Office before the author can sue for infringement, statutory damages, and attorneys' fees.

A copyright is essentially a government's legal protection of a person's basic property rights — the exclusive right to the work of one's mind.

7

Availability of Copyright Protection

Any work that is "fixed in a tangible form of expression" can be protected. The fixation need not be directly perceptible, so long as it may be communicated with the aid of a machine or device.

Some of the types of visual works commonly protected by copyright include:

- Advertisements
- Drawings
- Paintings
- Computer artwork
- Greeting cards
- Photographs
- Posters
- Original typography
- Symbols

- Graphic designs
- Technical drawings
- Architectural drawings
- Holograms
- Computer software
- Bumper stickers
- Cartoons
- Comic strips
- Characters
- Record jacket art
- Sculptures
- Various art prints

Works that cannot be protected by copyright include those that have not been fixed in a tangible form of expression, such as ideas, procedures, methods, principles, and so forth. (as distinguished from a written description or explanation, or an illustration). Also, works consisting entirely of information that is common property, such as purely factual information or data or cliches, and contains no original authorship cannot be protected.

Also, works consisting entirely of information that is common property and contains no original authorship cannot be protected.

Infringement is the illegal, intentional duplication, distribution, copying, or sale of a copyrighted work, or the preparation of a derivative work which is clearly based upon the idea expressed in an author's work. Specifically relating to art and graphic design, infringement is the usage and/or manipulation (changing any portion of a work) without the express written consent of the author.

An example of copyright infringement might be the copying (photocopying, scanning, and so forth) of all or a substantial portion of a photograph, work of art, or other type of authorship without the copyright holder's permission — even if it is not an exact copy.

Copyright infringement also includes scanning photographs and images from a publicly available source, such as a magazine or a stock photography book. Even if the scanned image is cropped, edited, tinted, manipulated, or otherwise altered so that the majority of the image has been changed, it still constitutes infringement.

When an author's exclusive work is used, in any way, without written permission, the infringer is liable for a variety of damages unless the use is a "fair use" or another legal defense applies. Sometimes, it is less expensive to acquire rights from the copyright owner up front, rather than to be forced to do so once the infringement has already occurred.

Defenses to Copyright Infringement

It is illegal for anyone to violate any of the rights provided to an author by the Copyright Act. However, Sections 107 through 119 of the Act state that copyrighted works may be used without the author's consent in a number of instances, the most significant three are:

1. Fair Use

   Fair use is essentially a provision that allows a person or organization to use a work without the author's permission for a purpose that does not compete with or injure the market for the work. An example might be an illustration in an article about the author's career or use of a client-assigned project in the author's portfolio. There is a great deal of case law analyzing different situations, and if you are in doubt about a specific situation, consult an attorney.

2. Compulsory License

   Permits a non-commercial, educational broadcasting station to use a published work without the author's consent. Rates of payment for such use are established by the Copyright Royalty Tribunal, and each station is required to publish a list of authors entitled to receive payment.

3. Public Domain

   When the term of a copyright expires, the material becomes part of the public domain, and anyone is free to use it.

Copyright Notification

While it is not necessary to insert the proper copyright notification (©1993 John Doe) on an item of original work to have it protected under the law, the author achieves important benefits by placing this notice on works:

It reduces or eliminates the vulnerability for "innocent infringement" and limits a defendant's ability to claim that he or she did not know that he or she infringed on a copyrighted work.

> **Copyright infringement also includes scanning photographs and images from a publicly available source, such as a magazine or a stock photography book.**

It is not necessary to register a work with the Copyright Office in order to assure protection under the law. However, registering a work also benefits the author.

1. Registering a work establishes a public record of the copyright claim.

2. Before an infringement suit may be filed in court, registration is necessary for works of U.S. origin and for foreign works not originating in a country that has adopted the Berne Convention.

3. If made before or within 5 years of publication, registration establishes evidence in court of the validity of the copyright and of the facts stated in the certificate.

4. If registration is made within 3 months after publication of the work, or prior to an infringement of the work, statutory damages and attorney's fees will be available to the copyright owner in court actions. Otherwise, only an award of actual damages and profits is available to the copyright owner, as well as an injunction against the infringer if a court deems it appropriate.

5. Registration allows the owner of the copyright to record the registration with the U.S. Customs Office for protection against the importation of infringing copies of the author's work.

Applying for a Copyright

To apply for a copyright on a work, the author must send the Register of Copyright:

1. The appropriate copyright form, available free of charge from the Copyright Office.

2. One or more copies of the actual work. More copies may be required, depending on the particular type of work.

3. The registration fee, currently $20.00 for each work.

The length of a copyright varies. A work created on or after January 1, 1978, is ordinarily protected for the author's lifetime plus 50 years after death.

Works for hire, anonymous, and pseudonymous works are protected for 75 years from the date of publication or 100 years from the date of their creation, whichever is shorter.

An author can register a work with the Copyright Office anytime within the life of the copyright, even after the work has been published. From the moment an original work is completed, it is considered an act of authorship, and the author legally owns the bundle of exclusive rights to the work.

Copyrights for Works Created for Hire

If a company or organization hires or contracts a person to produce an original work, copyright ownership and usage issues must be expressed in writing and signed by both parties. The law defines these types of relationships as "Work For Hire." In these cases, the party commissioning the work will be considered the owner, provided certain procedural steps are taken.

to be used, then the "work for hire" doctrine may not apply, and the artist/creator may retain both authorship recognition and copyright ownership.

For independent contractor agreement, there are four issues which must be addressed, negotiated, and agreed to in writing before work begins:

1. Whether or not the work is "work for hire."

2. Who shall retain legal copyright ownership of the work.

3. Who shall profit and in what proportions from any subsequent sale, licensing, rental, etc., or other usage of the work, for exhibition or use beyond the original scope of the project.

4. Confidentiality and/or nondisclosure agreements.

"You've done a thorough research job," Vincent remarked as he looked over my findings. "Not bad for a day at the library."

"Thanks. Even though I'm not a legal expert, I think I understand the fundamentals of copyright law," I said. "But with technology moving ahead so rapidly, it may create some copyright issues that we can't foresee yet."

"That's true," Vincent said. "As long as you respect the concept that an artist — no matter what kind — owns the rights to what he or she creates, you should have no problem."

Section 101 of the copyright statute defines a "work made for hire" as:

1. A work prepared by an employee within the scope of his or her employment.

2. A work specially ordered or commissioned for use as a contribution to a collective work, such as a motion picture, an instructional text, etc., if both parties expressly agree in a written document signed by them that the work shall be considered a "work made for hire."

The authors of a joint work are considered co-owners of the copyright in the work, unless there is a written agreement to the contrary. Copyright in each separate contribution to a periodical or other collective work is distinct from copyright in the collective work as a whole, and vests initially with the author of the contribution.

The lack of a written agreement which states specifically that the work is "made for hire," or if it is not signed by both parties, or if the above descriptions do not apply to the environment in which the work was created or is

2-D

An image that is constructed and exists in a two dimensional space having width and height. In geometric terms, it exists only on the x- and y-axes.

3-D

An image that is constructed in two dimensions, but is extruded into a third dimension. It has width, height, and depth, and it can be built, rotated, viewed, and manipulated from an infinite variety of perspectives. In geometric terms, it exists on the x-, y-, and z-axes.

Additive colors

Cyan, magenta, yellow, and black (CMYK). Red plus green forms yellow; red plus blue forms magenta, green plus blue forms cyan; red plus green plus blue forms white. Additive colors are used in the conventional 4-color printing process.

Algorithms

A well-defined series of mathematical and logical processes that can be applied to solve a problem in a finite number of steps. Used in computer programming.

Aliasing

The visual effect that occurs on a display screen whenever the degree of detail in the displayed image exceeds the resolution available on the output device.

Alpha channel

A soft-edged mask. The alpha channel assigns progressively decreasing color and transparency values in pixels, which permit one image to be composited over another with smooth edges and transparency where desired.

The alpha channel allows degrees of transparency to be adjusted in each color bit (channel) potentially independent of the

A

others. It also controls the anti-aliasing around the edge of an object when it is composited over another image.

Ambient light

The presence of illumination from all directions.

Anti-aliasing

The process of blurring the edges where one block of color meets another. Anti-aliasing sharpens an image by switching pixels to intermediate intensities along either side of the otherwise jagged diagonal lines.

Aspect ratio

The ratio of the frame width to the frame height. The standard aspect ratio of a TV frame is 4:3.

Bézier curves

Non-uniform curves which are defined by the positions of their endpoints and by two other points that indirectly define the tangents at the curve's endpoints. Usually, the tangent-defining points are not on the curve itself. The name is derived from Pierre Bézier, a French mathematician who pioneered the computer modeling of curved surfaces for Renault, the French auto manufacturer.

Binary code

The use of bits, a series of ones and zeros, to represent information that the computer can understand. The binary code assigns individual electronic switches within the computer to an on or off state. These switches control the processing actions within the computer.

Bit

One digit of the binary representation of a number — the fundamental unit of formal information. For example, 1101 is a 4-bit number. The word bit is a contraction of binary digit.

A

Bit level depth

In a frame buffer, the bit depth is a measure of color resolution. When there are more bits allocated to each pixel location, there are correspondingly more colors that can be displayed on the screen. A frame buffer 8 bits deep can store 256 colors. With an additional color look-up table (LUT), considerably more colors can be viewed.

Bit map

Information which contains a map of all the points to be displayed on a screen.

Bump mapping

One technique by which a surface texture can be applied to the representation of a realistic object on a graphics screen. In bump mapping, the surface normals of the object are perturbed; their direction in relation to the light vector is slightly altered according to a pre-determined degree. This technique is useful for consistent textures such as tire treads, carpet piles, and orange peel. It does not, however, affect the silhouette of the object and is not, therefore, universally useful.

Bus

A circuit over which data or power is transmitted to a number of locations. It is a common link, taking information from one or more sources to one or more destinations inside the computer.

Generally are three varieties of buses: 8-, 16-, and 32-bit, which contain 8, 16, and 32 parallel lines of data respectively. The higher the bus designation, the faster the computer can send information within the computer.

Byte

The smallest addressable unit in memory, made up of 8-bits and treated by

A

the computer as a single group. Industry measurement standards are:

• 1 kilobyte: 1,000 bytes

• 1 megabyte: 1,000,000 bytes

• 1 gigabyte: 1,000,000,000 bytes

Capacitor

A device for accumulating and holding a charge of electricity. In RAM, capacitors are used to hold live data, which includes information assigned to short term, rapidly accessible addresses.

Cartesian coordinates

The x and y coordinates that specify the position of a point on a plane and the x, y, and z coordinates that specify a point in a cube or spatial volume.

Cathode Ray Tube (CRT)

An electronic gun that emits a beam of electrons, illuminating phosphors on-screen as the beam repeatedly sweeps across the screen. Used both for computer monitors and television screens.

Central Processing Unit (CPU)

The computer within the computer which controls its internal storage, processing, and control circuitry.

Computer graphics

The creation, storage, and manipulation of models of objects and their pictures via a computer.

Constraints

Various types of accuracy aids that force interactive input into regular patterns. They are most often used for achieving exact correspondence of newly entered points, lines, or shapes with existing points, lines, or shapes on the screen,

A

and more importantly, in the data structure itself.

Constructive solid geometry

The process of creating a complex object by building smaller, simpler polygons, then combining them to form a solid.

Coordinate point

The spot on a CRT or other device which is identified by two series of x and y numbers.

Diffuse light

Light that originates from a specific source, but scatters in all directions.

Display list

A sequential list of instructions for vector graphics which is stored in the refresh buffer memory, in order to create a picture on a CRT.

Display memory

The memory device into which image data is mapped, representing graphic elements such as lines, shapes, dots, etc. that will be used to draw a designated image.

Display processor

An additional processor within the computer which takes over many of the calculations necessary to produce an image on a CRT.

Endpoints

In vector graphics, the points that specify each end of a line segment.

Expansion slots

Areas designated on a circuit board which allow the user to plug in a wide assortment of processing, input, and output hardware, such as modem, fax, and display cards.

Extrusion

The means by which a two-dimensional object is stretched into a three-dimensional one, adding the z axis.

Facets

In three-dimensional

A

modeling, polygons that comprise the surface of a computer-generated object. Facets also describe the flat surfaces that represent the connection of wireframe polygons.

Depending on the technical level of a program, facets can be subdivided into increasingly smaller sizes, to the point where, when rendered into a raster image, facets become invisible to the eye.

Curved surfaces can be represented by very small facets, which are later smoothed when the object is fully shaded.

Field

In television and raster graphics, one complete scan of a picture image from top to bottom.

Filter

A mask; a bit pattern which alters another bit pattern.

Fractal geometry

The description of intermediate shapes whose dimensionality need not be a whole number. Fractal dimensionality can express degrees of irregularities, and it is used in computer graphics for generating realistic simulations of natural formations such as mountains, coastlines, etc.

Frame buffer

A solid-state memory device for raster graphics that holds a matrix of digital values corresponding to the pixel pattern displayed or about to be displayed on the screen. The frame buffer permits the user to paint over an image, change the hue, saturation, and brightness, etc.

Gouraud shading

Intensity interpolation shading, named for its developer at Bell Labs. A

A

to jump to the nearest grid intersection whenever a point is entered.

four-step process involving the calculation of surface normals, vertex normals, and vertex intensities. Shading each polygon by linear interpolation of vertex intensities along each edge and between edges along scan lines. Gouraud shading gives a convincing appearance of smooth shading and the illusion of a curved surface, even though the model is composed of flat polygons.

Grid constraint

An accuracy aid that causes the screen cursor

Hidden line / Hidden surface algorithms

The step-by-step mathematical procedure that is required to conceal normally hidden lines and surfaces, but which a computer will display unless otherwise instructed.

Image processing

The enhancement of a picture obtained from external sources, which is converted into digital information and augmented by either the user (i.e., adding or changing tints, colors, etc.), or by pre-programmed instructions (i.e. images sent back from space probes).

Input devices

Any physical device which translates a user's intentions into information that the computer can understand and process. These include stylus, hand cursor, data tablet, function switches, control dials, keyboard, light pen, joystick, track ball, touch-sensitive screen, and mouse.

Interactive graphics system

A computer graphics system that requests and accepts input from a user

A

refreshed first, followed by the even-numbered scan lines.

and enables the user to direct the processing operations according to the requirements of a specific graphics task.

Interface

The boundary at which two components of a computer system meet. The term may also be used to describe the communication between a user and an interactive computer system.

Interlaced

A process for refreshing an image on the screen that reduces flicker. Odd-numbered scan lines are

Interpolation

The determination of a value that lies between two known values through mathematical calculation. In computer graphics, this process is, often applied to creating curves by joining a series of straight line segments, or to defining smoothing curves between specific points. Given beginning and ending points, interpolation calculates the internal points along a smooth gradient. Interpolation is basically still-form metamorphosis, in which all intermediate shapes are defined along a path between two objects.

Iteration

The repetitive performance of a processing task.

Iterative routine

A process that repeatedly performs a series of steps (iterations) making successive, increasingly accurate approximations until obtaining a specified condition.

Lofting

An interactive graphics technique in which the third dimension is obtained from a two-dimensional representation, as in elevating the

A

contours of a topographical map. Lofting is another term used to describe the extrusion process.

Look Up Table (LUT)

A small piece of memory (often within a frame buffer) that contains color content values.

Luminance

A psychophysical measurement of perceived radiant power, expressed in candles per square meter. Luminance values are ultimately derived from observations of a standard light source by a large number of people, to which other light sources are then compared. It has been well established that the human eye is a very good judge of relatively stronger or weaker sources of light. As a result, electronic instruments can be calibrated to match human responses, thus providing a wide range of luminosity measurements.

Memory planes

A description of the several layers of instructions to display raster images when more than two colors are used in the image. These subdivisions of a computer memory usually correspond with the contents of each plane. For example, a frame buffer may have several memory planes, each one holding a complete image for display on a CRT.

Microprocessor

Essentially a computer on a chip, also known as the brain inside the computer and the heart of the central processing unit. The microprocessor acquires, processes, and sequences the input and output of millions of bits of data each second. A microprocessor represents the physical reduction of more than a mil-

A

lion transistors and other components from an early circuit board into microscopic proportions.

Physically larger early computers consisted of hundreds of thousands of individual transistors, manually wired together to process the binary information needed to complete a wide range of processing assignments. The microprocessor is a complete, microscopic version of the early full-size computer. The power of a microprocessor is determined by the number of components reduced and assembled into it, which affects the speed with which it can process information.

Mass-produced from silicon through a photo-chemical process, micro-processors are also known as microchips and integrated circuits. Manufacturers are currently experimenting with X-rays to fit even more transistors onto individual chips.

Model

The geometry that is electronically constructed on a computer graphics system.

Moving point constraints

Additions to key frames that specify curves in time and space. These constrain path and speed of points within key frames. A patch network serves as the in-between wireframes between two key frames.

Output devices

Any device that produces tangible copies of digital information. These include pen plotter, electro-static printer/plotter, laser printer, ink jet printer, impact printer/plotter, non-impact printer/plotter, photographic recorder, and film recorder.

A

Parallel port

A port that supports synchronous, high-speed data flow along parallel lines to external devices such as printers. A parallel port is basically an extension of the computer's internal data bus.

Parallel processing

The process of increasing a computer's processing speed by enabling it to perform many calculations simultaneously.

Patches

Free-form sculpted surfaces that may be combined with other models to form a whole. The name refers to the appearance of a complex patchwork in a geometric model.

Phong shading

A sophisticated shading model used in realistic three-dimensional representations. Created by Bui-Tuong Phong, it discovers the surface normals in the object at each vertex, then interpolates further surface normals for each point across the face of each polygon. Each of these is then compared to the direction of the light source in order to calculate the brightness of the point. The end result is smooth shading for curved surfaces, complete with accurate highlights.

Pixel

Groups of tiny dots of phosphor on a CRT that, when illuminated as a group, form the smallest distinguishable unit of a raster display. A raster display of 1280x1024 pixels contains well over a million points with which to represent the image on the screen.

Polygon

A shape formed by three or more connected lines, enclosing an area. A poly-

A

Random Access Memory
(RAM)

A temporary storage place for information regularly accessed by the user during operations on a specific program or programs. RAM provides virtually instantaneous access to any of the information stored within it.

A certain amount of RAM is necessary to archive and retrieve information the CPU might need to access. The more RAM available, the more information a program can use at a given time. RAM is essentially an electronic hard drive, with an electrical current constantly maintaining, reading, and writing information. As a result, all data held in RAM is

lost forever when the computer is turned off.

Raster display

Displays a parallel array of horizontal lines into which picture information is inserted, starting at the top of the screen and gradually working its way to the bottom. This technology is used for computer monitors and television screens.

Raster graphic

An image created with a collection of small, separate dots. Also known as a bitmapped graphic.

gon is one of the standard graphics primitives.

Port

An input/output device that controls the flow of data to and from the CPU and external devices such as printers and modems. Also known as an interface.

Primitives

Basic graphical entities, such as points, line segments, and polygons that can be geometrically oriented in two or three dimensions.

A

Ray tracing

A technique for creating realistic computer images by tracing rays from a viewpoint to the light source, a reverse path of light rays. The algorithm used calculates both hidden surfaces and shading, and it requires tremendous processing power to generate an image.

Real-time

A term used to describe the speed at which a computer will process and display information at the user's own speed. In real-time, input is immediately processed with no delay.

Refresh buffer memory

Used in vector systems to hold a display list of plotting commands.

Refresh cycle

The process of writing and rewriting an image to a CRT at least 30 times per second.

Rendering

The process of converting a vector-based graphic into a raster-based graphic. Computationally intensive, rendering requires all the RAM and processing speed available on the computer.

Resolution

Refers to three factors: the picture data description, the device memory, and the display surface. Resolution is typically expressed in x and y terms, where x represents the number of horizontal pixels, and represents the number of vertical pixels. Additional descriptions are added to refer to the bit depth of each pixel (512x512x256 colors). Three levels of resolution are generally accepted:
Low: 512x512 or below
Medium: 1,024x1,024
High: 2,048x2,048 or above

A

and external devices such as printers, modems, and even other computers.

Shading models

The process of turning a vector image into a raster image. Shading models provide mathematical descriptions of how objects reflect ambient, diffused, and specular light. Solid objects are modeled by a series of connected polygons.

In three-dimensional computer graphics modeling, objects can be given the appearance of solidity by introducing one or more light sources, then recalculating the intensity of each pixel representing the object. Those pixels representing facets of the object that are inclined toward the light source will be brighter than those on facets in the shaded area. This is a complex problem, involving many related considerations including the type of light, texture, geometry, and shadows cast from other objects.

Sketching

Freehand drawing of lines and colors with an interactive display.

Small Computer Systems Interface (SCSI)

Popularly known as the scuzzy interface. The SCSI is typically a flat

Higher resolution images therefore require more memory.

Resolution is further divided into spatial and radiometric resolution. Spatial resolution is the number of pixels used to render an image. Radiometric resolution is the number of bits per pixel that are available to indicate intensity values.

Serial port

A port that synchronizes and makes asynchronous data transmission easier between the computer

A

plastic ribbon cable inside which wires run side by side so that any wire can be reached at any point. The SCSI interface allows a wide variety of peripheral hardware to be plugged into the computer, and it allows computers and peripherals to exchange data. The SCSI interface is connected to a plug-in port at the back of the computer.

Software

Computer-readable code that presents a consistent interface to the user. Software acts as the intermediary between the user and computer hardware, enabling the user to perform multiple tasks. Software includes graphic, image manipulation, word processing, spreadsheet, and game programs among many others.

Specular light

Light that originates from a specific source, but bounces off of an object mainly in one direction. It may, to some extent, be diffused on a rough surface. The angle of reflectance equals the angle of incidence.

Sphere

A solid round body, the surface of which is everywhere equidistant from the center.

Splines

Smooth curves that are fitted to a series of arbitrarily defined points. Prior to the development of Computer-Aided Design (CAD) systems, drafters used flexible rulers to create these curves. With CAD, splines are generated automatically.

Subtractive colors

Red, green, blue (RGB). Yellow and magenta subtract from white to form red; yellow and cyan subtract from white to form green; cyan and magenta

to a tangent plane touching the surface at the point of touch.

subtract from white to form blue. The subtractive process is used to display colors on a CRT.

Surface modeling

One of the three broad categories of three-dimensional modeling in which the surfaces of objects are defined by connecting surface elements to the edge model.

Surface normals

A line perpendicular to a surface. It may be at a right angle to a plane or, in the case of a curved surface, at a right angle

Texture mapping

The process of providing modeled surfaces with characteristic textures while not having to define every individual irregularity.

Vector graphic

An image created from mathematical formulas that define the directional lines composing the image. Also known as object-oriented graphics, vector images do not require a frame buffer. They can be moved and resized at will.

Vector graphics, because they are created from lines of code, require little RAM to process.

Vertex

In geometry, the point of intersection of the two lines forming an angle; it is the point of a triangle farthest from and opposite to the line chosen as a base.

Virtual memory

The process of assigning a designated section of the hard disk as a portion of RAM for processing tasks that exceed a computer's RAM. It allows a computer to process more information, but because it is an electro-

A

mechanical process of sending and receiving— as opposed to RAM, which is strictly electronic — virtual memory takes longer to process.

Wireframe model

A model composed of lines built one at a time, or a solid object that is composed one shape at a time.

CONTRIBUTING ARTISTS

Jeff Brice Pages 119, 121, 122, 123, 139, 143

Mark Jasin Pages 114, 115, 117, 118, 142

Louis Katz Pages 4, 15, 17, 21, 32, 33, 35, 41, 44, 45, 47, 49, 52, 56, 57, 62, 66, 104

Kory Kredit Pages 1, 5, 19, 25, 37, 68

Chad M. Little Pages 8, 9, 11, 14, 24, 28, 29, 39, 59, 70, 109, 146

Ron Scott Pages 132, 133, 134, 135

Tery Spataro Page 108

Brian Stauffer Pages 126, 127, 128, 129, 130

Paul Zwolak, represented by Marlena Torzecka Page 105

BIBLIOGRAPHY

Computer Animation Chronology, Rosebush, Judson, SIGGRAPH Video Review, 1988.

American Dreams: One Hundred Years of Business Ideas and Innovation from The Wall Street Journal, Morris, Kenneth, Robinson, Marc, and Kroll, Richard, Lightbulb Press, 1991.

Animation Techniques, Noake, Roger, Chartwell Books, 1988.

The Art of David Em, Ross, David A. and Em, David, 1988.

Business and Legal Forms for Graphic Designers, Crawford, Tad and Bruck, Eva Doman, New York: Allworth Press, 1990.

Computer Graphics, Lewell, John, Orbis Publishing, 1985.

Computer Graphics: Principles & Practice, Foley, VanDam, Feiner, and Hughes, Addison-Wesley Publishing, Second Edition, 1990.

Computer Images, Time-Life Books, 1986.

Copyright Basics (Circular 1), *Duration of Copyright* (Circular 15a), United States Copyright Office, Library of Congress, Washington, D.C. 20559; Forms hotline: 202-707-9100; Public Information Office: 202-707-3000.

Copyright Law (video), Association for Information Media and Equipment.

Copyright Primer, American Library Association, 1987.

Copyright: Principles, Law, and Practice, Goldstein, Paul, Foundation Press, 1989.

Digital Visions, Goodman, Cynthia, Times Mirror, 1987.

Eureka! An Illustrated History Of Inventions From The Wheel To The Computer, DeBono, Edward, Thames and Hudson, 1974.

How Computers Really Work, White, Jack, Dodd, Mead, & Company, 1986.

How Computers Work, White, Ron, Ziff-Davis Publishing, 1993.

C

Que's Computer User's Dictionary, Pfaffenberger, Bryan, Carmel, IN: Que Corporation, Third Edition, 1992.

The Software Developer's Legal Guide, Fishman, Stephen, Berkeley, CA: Nolo Press, 1994.

The Triumph Of Invention: A History Of Man's Technological Genius, Williams, Trevor I., MacDonald & Co., 1988.

How to Sell Your Photographs and Illustrations, Gordon, Elliott and Barbara, New York: Allworth Press, 1990.

Legal Guide for the Visual Artist, Crawford, Tad, New York: Allworth Press, 1989.

Licensing Art and Design, Leland, Caryn R., New York: Allworth Press, 1990.

Make It Legal, Rossol, Monona, New York: Allworth Press, 1990.

Protecting Your Rights & Increasing Your Income (audio cassette), Crawford, Tad, New York: Allworth Press.

ABOUT THE CD-ROM

You can immediately begin exploring the concepts you've learned in this book through this special CD-ROM. The *Becoming a Computer Artist* CD-ROM includes

• A special demo version of RIO©, the powerful graphics application from AT&T Multimedia Software Solutions.

• Images and supporting files for the artwork created in Chapter 4.

• A preview of the *Becoming a Computer Artist* multimedia software.

RIO Demo

RIO is professional illustration, image design, and presentation software for DOS. It lets you manipulate and enhance scanned images or create original illustrations using a variety of design and creation tools. It combines the functions of a vector program with the ability to place raster images and manipulate them to some degree.

RIO takes full advantage of true-color displays by using 16.7 million colors, and it uses a pixel's alpha channel to create specialized imaging effects with transparency and image matting.

This special version has nearly all the capabilities of the full-featured RIO program available from AT&T. However, this version cannot render high-resolution raster images such as Targa files, and you are limited to ten saves of any file.

Installing RIO

To install the RIO working model, insert the CD-ROM into your drive and follow these steps:

1. Make sure your DOS mouse driver is installed. Consult the mouse manufacturer's documentation if you need further instructions.

2. At the DOS prompt, type: D:\INSTALL and press Enter. If your CD-ROM is not drive D, substitute the appropriate drive letter. For example, if your CD-ROM drive is drive F, type F:\INSTALL.

3. When the installation program begins, it will display license information for the software. Follow the installation instructions shown on the screen to continue.

4. When the last screen of license information has been displayed, use the arrow keys to highlight "I agree" and press Enter.

5. Highlight the drive where you want to install the software and press Enter.

6. The default installation directory is \RIODEMO. You can change this, or you can press Enter to accept the default directory.

7. Choose whether to install the "16-color VGA" or "VESA VGA" version of RIO, and press Enter. If you want to display more than 16 colors, you must choose the "VESA VGA" option and you must have a VESA-compatible video card.

8. Choose whether to use a mouse, a tablet or both, and then press Enter.

9. Choose which output devices to install, and press Enter.

D

Once you've installed the 16-color VGA version or the VESA VGA version of the software, you must re-install RIO if you wish to change versions.

10. Press a key, and the install program will begin installing the RIO demo software to your hard drive.

To start the working model of RIO (after it's been installed), change to the \RIODEMO directory (type CD \RIODEMO and press Enter), Type RIO and press Enter. If you changed the name of this directory during the installation, substitute that name in the CD command.

Important Notes

You can save scenes, objects, images, and styles up to 10 times. To save these files, use the Files option (not the Save or Save As) on the Control menu and select the save option you want.

To display 16- or 24-bit color, your VGA board must have its VESA BIOS extensions loaded before starting RIO. Refer to your VGA board's documentation regarding VESA display modes.

In RIO, the left mouse button is used to Select, and the right button is used to cancel operations. Use the left button to select items, initiate commands, etc., and the right button to cancel, restore, etc. These are general instructions; you must use the right button to access an object's attributes menu once the object is selected.

RIO refers to the Escape key as the Cancel key or Cancel command.

Special offer

AT&T Multimedia Software Solutions will begin marketing Windows 3.1 versions of its products for the small office/home office and consumer markets, as well as Windows NT versions for the professional market. As a special promotion with this book, AT&T is offering a 50% discount off the manufacturer's suggested retail price of its DOS products, or the new Windows 3.1 or Windows NT products when they are available.

You must provide proof of purchase of this book to receive the discount. This can be the advertisement for RIO, found near the end of the book. You must submit the original, not a copy.

Call 1-800-448-6727 (407-662-7309 direct line) to place an order or for more information. This special promotion is only available directly from AT&T Multimedia Software Solutions.

Since the working model is a demo, AT&T is not offering free technical support. Documentation is available, however, at a minimal cost. You can order a Guide to the working model (a tutorial and menu map) for $15 plus tax. A full set of product documentation costs $75 plus tax.

Images and Supporting Files

These files represent the artwork created in Chapter 4 of the book. You can access the vector scene files (.SCN)—some of which contain raster images—in RIO. You'll also

D

find the in-progress raster files and the final high resolution raster files for the four images created in Chapter 4.

Please note that these images are included on the CD for educational purposes only. Do not attempt to use, tamper with, or change them in any way, in accordance with the copyright issues presented in Chapter 7.

Presentation

This presentation is a preview of the full-scale multimedia version of *Becoming a Computer Artist.* More than just a story, the multimedia version is an experience that takes you inside the warehouse where Vincent comes to life. Meet the people who shaped the computer graphics industry and the technologies they developed. Learn computer graphics fundamentals through easy-to-understand, step-by-step lessons.

See how computer-generated animation and video can explain concepts and demonstrate theories with powerful, memorable images. And explore a complete reference library of computer graphics associations, trade shows, and other useful information. This interactive guide will give you an important head start in becoming a computer artist.

For more information on the interactive version of this book, please call 1-800-897-3637.

I N D E X

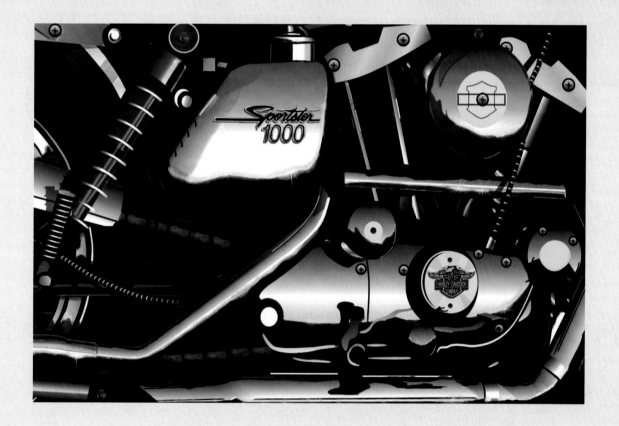

THE CD-ROM

You can immediately begin exploring the concepts you've learned in *Becoming a Computer Artist* through this special PC format CD-ROM. The *Becoming a Computer Artist* CD-ROM includes

● A special demo version of RIO©, the professional graphics application from AT&T Multimedia Software Solutions. RIO lets you manipulate and enhance scanned images or create original illustrations using a variety of design and creation tools.

This special working model has nearly all the capabilities of the full-featured RIO program, except this version cannot render high-resolution raster images such as Targa files and you can save scenes, objects, images, and styles up to ten times.

● Images and supporting files for the artwork created in Chapter 4, including vector scene files (.SCN) for RIO, in-progress images and high-resolution final images.

● A preview of the full-scale multimedia version of *Becoming a Computer Artist*.

To install the RIO working model, insert the CD-ROM into your drive and follow these steps:

1. Make sure your DOS mouse driver is installed. Consult the mouse manufacturer's documentation if you need further instructions.

2. At the DOS prompt, type: D:\INSTALL and press Enter. If your CD-ROM is not drive D, substitute the appropriate drive letter. For example, if your CD-ROM drive is drive F, type F:\INSTALL.

3. When the installation program begins, it will display license information for the software. Follow the installation instructions shown on the screen to continue.

4. The installation program will guide you through the remaining steps of the process.

When the installation program is complete, you can start RIO. Change to the \RIO directory of your hard drive, type RIO and press Enter. See Appendix D, "About the CD-ROM," for more information on using this software and for more detailed installation instructions.

To setup the software for the presentation on the interactive *Becoming a Computer Artist* software, insert the CD-ROM into your drive and follow these steps:

1. Start up Microsoft Windows (version 3.1 or higher).

2. From Program Manager or File Manager, select **F**ile + **R**un from the menu.

3. Type D:\SETUP and press Enter. If your CD-ROM is not drive D, substitute the appropriate drive letter. For example, if your CD-ROM drive is drive F, type F:\SETUP.

4. Follow the instructions shown on the screen. This program will set up a Program Manager group named *Becoming A Computer Artist*.

5. When the setup program has completed, the Microsoft Video for Windows 1.1 installation program will begin. This will install the run-time files needed for playing video within Windows.

To start the demo, double-click on the Book Demo icon in the *Becoming A Computer Artist* group in Program Manager.

Minimum System Requirements: 386 or better processor, VGA or SVGA graphics, and a Microsoft-compatible mouse. VESA VGA compatible graphics card needed for displaying more than 16 colors.